DILAPIDATIONS IN SCOTLAND

DILAPIDATIONS IN SCOTLAND

Malcolm F. Fleming, B.A., L.LB.,

Solicitor

W. GREEN/Sweet & Maxwell
EDINBURGH
1997

First published 1997

© 1997
W. GREEN & SON LTD

ISBN 0 414 01183 X

No natural forests were destroyed to make this product;
only farmed timber was used and replanted

A CIP catalogue reference for this book is available from the British Library

Typeset by Trinity Typesetting, Edinburgh
Printed in Great Britain by Redwood Books, Wiltshire

CONTENTS

Chapter 6: Residential Leases

Chapter 7: Agricultural Tenancies

PREFACE

This book is primarily intended to deal with leases of commercial property in Scotland but includes chapters on residential and agricultural tenancies and the obligations relating to repairs contained or implied in such leases. The coverage of those leases is, however, given less prominence.

The book is intended to be of benefit primarily to solicitors in private practice but has also been written to some extent with the needs of the surveying profession in mind. Members of the legal profession will therefore excuse the inclusion of some statements of the common law which they might, perhaps, consider to be so well known as to be not worth repeating.

I would like to express my grateful thanks to my former partner, Ian Inglis, for generally reading and commenting upon the text and giving particularly helpful advice on the sections of the book dealing with damages; to my partner, Ian Stubbs, and his colleague, Timothy Conduit, for their very helpful contributions in relation to the chapters on residential and agricultural tenancies; and last but not least to my secretary, Maud Keating, for typing and correcting the text.

The book attempts to set out the law as at April 1, 1997. Any errors and omissions are those of the author.

TABLE OF CASES

TABLE OF STATUTES

STATUTORY INSTRUMENTS

CHAPTER 1

COMMON LAW AND STATUTE AFFECTING REPAIRS

Implied obligations at common law

Unless modified by the particular lease or by statute, where premises **1.1** are let in Scotland the landlord impliedly warrants that they are fit for the purpose for which they are let and in tenantable condition. The implied warranty of fitness for purpose can be and usually is removed in commercial leases by a statement in the lease that the tenant "accepts the premises as in proper tenantable condition" (or words to that effect).[1] In a recent case it has been held that this implied warranty as to fitness for purpose applies, in the case of a multi-let building, not only to the actual premises let but also to the common parts and structure of the building.[2]

Again, unless modified by the lease or statute, a landlord at **1.2** common law is obliged to keep the premises in a tenantable condition and wind and watertight.[3] During the course of his judgment in *Wolfson v. Forrester*,[4] Lord President Dunedin stated:

"By the Law of Scotland the lease of every urban tenement is, in default of any specific stipulation, deemed to include an obligation on the part of the Landlord to hand over the premises in a wind and water tight condition, and if he does not do so there is a breach of contract and he may be liable in damages. He is also bound to put them into a wind and water tight condition if by accident they become not so. But this is not a warranty, and accordingly he is in no breach as to this part of his bargain till the defect is brought to his notice and he fails to remedy it."

---

[1] *Turner's Trs. v. Steel* (1900) 2 F. 363.
[2] *Blackwell v. Farmfoods (Aberdeen) Ltd,* 1991 G.W.D. 4–219. See para. 2.15.
[3] *Johnstone v. Hugham* (1894) 21 R. 777 where the tenant successfully sued the landlord for having been denied use of the premises because of the landlord's failure to carry out repairs necessitated by natural decay.
[4] 1910 S.C. 675 at p. 680, but see para. 4.1 for the more onerous obligation upon a landlord when the item to be repaired is within the landlord's control (*e.g.* the structure of multi-let building) and not in the tenant's exclusive possession.

The tenant therefore has very little liability for repairs at common law and this explains why the repairing clause in Scottish leases tends to go further than the equivalent in an English lease so as to transfer the whole repairing liability on to the tenant.[5] This topic is dealt with in more detail in Chapter 2. As an example at this stage, it will be sufficient to know that although in *Turners' Trustees v. Steel*[6] the tenant accepted the premises as in proper tenantable condition and repair and bound himself to leave them in good tenantable condition and repair, the tenant was held not liable for repairs which became necessary as a result of inevitable decay caused by lapse of time or wear and tear.

1.3   With the exception of residential and agricultural leases which are dealt with in Chapters 6 and 7, there is very little statute which upsets the common law position stated in paragraphs 1.1 and 1.2. Scotland is perhaps fortunate in not having equivalents of the English Landlord and Tenant Acts of 1927, 1954 and 1988, the Law of Property Act 1925, the Leasehold Property (Repairs) Act 1938 or the Defective Premises Act 1972. There are of course numerous statutes which have a bearing on what the tenant may have to do in using the premises — such as the Occupiers Liability (Scotland) Act 1960, the Factories Act 1961, the Offices, Shops and Railway Premises Act 1968, the Health and Safety at Work etc. Act 1974, the Environmental Protection Act 1990, the Clean Air Act 1993, the Environment Act 1995 and doubtless numerous others, but these only have an indirect bearing on the topic. Although the Housing Grants, Construction and Regeneration Act 1996, sections 104 and 105, are drawn widely enough to suggest that certain aspects of a lease (*e.g.* the painting and decorating obligations) may be regarded as a construction contract, at the time of going to press little comment has been made in the legal journals as to the impact on leases of these sections. It would however appear that the direct impact of the Act on commercial leases may be quite limited. Accordingly, in almost all cases affecting the subject of dilapidations, the text of a lease of commercial property can be read as meaning what it says subject to the overriding requirement of common law.

---

[5] For a further exposition of the landlord's implied obligations at common law, see Paton and Cameron, *The Law of Landlord and Tenant in Scotland*, pp. 130 *et seq.* and Rankine, *The Law of Leases in Scotland*, (3rd ed., 1916), pp. 240 *et seq.*

[6] (1900) 2 F. 363.

CHAPTER 2

TENANT'S OBLIGATIONS TO REPAIR UNDER PROVISIONS OF THE LEASE OR CONTRACT

Relevant documentation

Assuming that the matter is governed by the provisions of the lease **2.1** or contract, the first task of the adviser of the landlord or the tenant is to examine the leasehold documentation. The original lease may have been modified by numerous amending documents, especially minutes of variation, assignations (which frequently effect changes to the lease itself), licences for works and similar documents. All of these must be assembled and checked to ascertain their impact on the relevant provisions which affect the liability of the tenant or the landlord to effect repairs.

Is the tenant liable in terms of the lease?

Before the tenant can be liable for carrying out repairs (or for failure **2.2** to do so) three main factors must concur:

(1) There has to be a binding contract of lease between the parties.

(2) The description of the premises let to the tenant must cover or include the item which the landlord is seeking to have the tenant repair (or there must be some other specific provision in the lease dealing with the matter).

(3) The repairing clause or some other clause in the lease must cover or include the obligation which the landlord is seeking to enforce.

These factors are now examined in more detail.

Is there a binding contract of lease?

In Scotland a lease for a year or less does not need to be in writing. **2.3** Since it may be very difficult to establish their terms, this work does not deal with such leases. A lease for more than a year must be in writing and must, if entered into prior to the passing of the Requirements of Writing (Scotland) Act 1995, be signed by the parties in what was known as "probative" form, *i.e.* usually before two witnesses in the case of an individual person and by two directors, or one director and the secretary, or two authorised signatories, in the case of companies. The Requirements of Writing (Scotland) Act 1995 altered the rules relating to execution of documents and a lease for more than a year will be validly executed if merely signed by an individual or if merely signed by a director, the secretary or an authorised signatory on behalf of a company. Although leases executed in this manner after the 1995 Act are valid and binding, they are not "self proving" (in other words, their execution may have to be established in court if challenged) and cannot be registered in the Books of Council and Session. Since there are technical advantages in having leases so registered (which are beyond the scope of this work) leases of any significant duration are almost invariably in "self proving" form. This requires that the signature of an individual or the single signature on behalf of a company must be witnessed by one witness. In the case of a company, there are alternatives, such as signature by two authorised signatories or the signature by one authorised signatory plus the affixing of the company seal. There are numerous other technical requirements and exceptions to these main rules but they are beyond the scope of this work.[1]

2.4 The contract of lease also has to comply with the basic requirements of the common law of leases in Scotland; it must therefore:

  (1) identify the landlord and tenant;
  (2) identify the premises let;
  (3) contain a definite rent; and,
  (4) have a specific duration.[2]

If it does not comply with all of these requirements, then although it might constitute another form of contract, it will not be a lease. For example, if no specific premises are identified of which the tenant is entitled to exclusive possession, the contract may be a

---

[1] See, *e.g.* Paton and Cameron, *The Law of Landlord and Tenant in Scotland,* pp. 28 *et seq.* and pp. 88, 89 and *Stair Memorial Encyclopaedia on The Laws of Scotland,* Vol. 13, paras. 135 *et seq.* on what used to be known as homologation and *rei interventus,* two terms now abolished and redefined by s. 1 of the Requirements of Writing (Scotland) Act 1995.

[2] See Paton and Cameron, *op.cit.,* pp. 5 *et seq.*

licence personal between the original contracting parties as where an in-store concession arrangement simply allows the licensee to occupy an area of so many square metres as made available to him from time to time by the landlord.[3] Originally even contracts of lease were regarded in Scots law as personal between the original contracting parties so that, for instance, a new owner in succession to the landlord could evict the tenant. However, by the Leases Act of 1449, it was provided that a lease is binding against successors in title of the original landlord if:

(1) it is in writing (if for more than one year);
(2) it provides for a specific continuing rent;
(3) it has a definite expiry date; and,
(4) the tenant has actually entered into physical possession of the property.[4]

This last requirement (of possession) is unnecessary if the lease has been recorded in the Register of Sasines or in the Land Register of Scotland, that being regarded as equivalent to possession. However, for that to be possible the lease has to be for more than 20 years.

2.5 The landlord, if the lease is a head lease, will normally transmit his interest to a successor by a conveyance of the ownership of the property to the new owner. A tenant, on the other hand (and the landlord too, if his interest is also leasehold, *e.g.* under a head lease), will normally transmit his interest by assignation of the relevant leasehold interest. Such an assignation of course has to be permitted by the terms (whether express or implied at common law) of the lease being assigned.

2.6 If the lease being examined is a binding lease and complies with the provisions of the Leases Act 1449 it should be capable of being enforced by and between the proper successors in title of both the original landlord and original tenant. It is also possible that previous tenants could be liable if the obligations undertaken by the original tenant were held to have been undertaken jointly and severally with successor tenants (with results somewhat akin to those of privity of contract in England) and also that guarantors may be liable. These topics are outwith the scope of this book.

---

[3] See *Stair Memorial Encyclopaedia on The Laws of Scotland*, Vol. 13, paras 120, 771.
[4] For more details on this topic see Paton and Cameron, *op.cit.*, pp. 103 *et seq.*

Description of the premises

2.7 Assuming that the repairing obligation sought to be enforced by the landlord relates to the premises as defined in the lease, the next matter to be checked is the precise definition and description of the premises. This is normally contained near the beginning of the lease either at length or by reference to a schedule containing the description. It ought to go without saying that even if there is a ferociously comprehensive and watertight repairing obligation upon the tenant in the lease in question, it will not assist the landlord one iota if the item which the landlord seeks to have the tenant repair is not covered by the definition of the premises or if there is room for debate on the point. The author's experience, however, is that in preparing schedules of dilapidations, landlords or their agents often ignore this either in error or perhaps deliberately! Since almost all obligations which the tenant assumes in the lease relate to the premises as defined, the description of the premises is the first place the agent for the tenant should look to see whether the tenant is liable or not. The subject of fittings and fixtures is dealt with in Chapter 3.

Single occupancy leases

2.8 The description of the premises is simplest in what is known as a "single occupancy" lease — *i.e.* one where the tenant has a lease of the *whole* of the landlord's property. Examples of this kind of lease include:

(1) The whole of the building plus its site and surrounding ground, *e.g.* a detached warehouse and yard.

(2) The whole of a shopping centre or industrial complex; this type of property will often be the subject of a ground lease (which will nonetheless frequently contain repairing obligations upon the tenant) to an institution which will itself grant what are known as "multi-occupational" leases to occupying sub-tenants.

(3) The landlord's entire interest in a traditional old tenement building. This interest often consists of a ground floor shop or perhaps an upper storey office within such a tenement.

In such "single occupancy" leases, the description is very often by reference to the landlord's own title. In other words, the landlord lets to the tenant the entire extent of what the landlord himself owns. This has the disadvantage that one then has to examine the landlord's own title to see what is let, but the significant advantage, from the landlord's perspective, is that since everything the landlord owns has been let, there should be nothing which the landlord remains liable to repair — provided the lease contains a comprehensive repairing clause.

Where a single occupancy lease consists of the landlord's entire **2.9** interest in a traditional old tenement building, the description in the landlord's title will normally take one of two forms:

(1) A brief description of the flat or shop itself (*e.g.* "the southmost flat on the first floor above the ground floor of the tenement building known as numbers 10, 12 and 14 High Street, Anytown, in the County of Lanark"), often without a plan, except sometimes in the case of shops, *together with* a right in common with the other owners in the tenement to the solum or ground on which the tenement is built, the amenity ground belonging to it, foundations, outside and gable walls, roof and common service media, etc. Such a title will normally provide that the owner of each flat is responsible for maintaining that flat and allocate the share of the costs of repairs to tenement property held in common for which each proprietor is liable.

(2) An equally brief description of the flat or shop itself (as in 1 above) but without any specified common rights.

In a lease based on the description in the landlord's title taking **2.10** the form of the first example in paragraph 2.9, the description will, or should, carry with it the landlord's common rights in the tenement. In a lease based upon the description of the landlord's title taking the form of the second example in paragraph 2.9, the common law of tenement will flesh out what the landlord is deemed to own in the tenement (and therefore the extent of the premises let by the lease). Common law broadly provides that:

(1) the owner of each flat owns that part of the outside or main walls which surrounds or bounds the flat; as far as gable walls are concerned they are common to the flat owners on either side of them;

(2) the owner of the lowest flat in the tenement owns the foundations of the tenement, so far as they lie beneath the flat concerned and also any ground lying *ex adverso* (*i.e.* opposite and adjacent to) that flat;

(3) the owner of the top flat owns the roof of the tenement so far as situated above the flat concerned;

(4) the common passages and stairs belong in common to the proprietors of the flats to which they give access, the surrounding

walls being the common property of those properties and of the owner of the flat (if any) on the other side of the relevant wall; and,

(5) the boundary between flats is the centre line of the joists separating them.

Whilst the ownership is thus split at common law, common law also provides that each of the owners in the tenement has a common interest in the main structural parts of the tenement so that the owner of each can be compelled to uphold the property which he owns so far as necessary to support or prevent injury to the property of the other owners in the tenement. The owner may also be prevented from making certain alterations.[5]

Multiple occupancy leases

2.11 Whilst, except in the case of flatted property, the description of premises in single occupation is relatively straightforward to check, the description of premises in a building or a group of buildings owned by one landlord but let as separate units to numerous tenants by what has come to be known as a multiple occupancy lease is, or ought to be, considerably more sophisticated. The normal scheme of such leases is that the landlord retains and remains responsible for the main structure and parts of the building used in common by the various tenants, his costs being recovered from those tenants by a service charge (see Chapter 4). A normal method of achieving this requires that the description of the premises in, for example, a multistorey office building owned by a single landlord will:

(1) describe the location of the premises as being on the relevant floor of the building and show their approximate extent by reference to a suitable floor plan;

(2) exclude from the definition of the premises all structural and common parts of the building (*e.g.* columns, floor slabs or joists, main walls, common passages, etc.) and common services although the tenant will normally be given common rights in relation to such of these are necessary for his enjoyment and use of the premises;

(3) include in the definition non-structural walls, floor and ceiling finishes, etc.

---

[5] See Gloag and Henderson, *Introduction to the Law of Scotland*, (9th ed., 1987), para. 40.18 for a simple but fuller explanation of the common law of tenement.

Thus what is let (and what the tenant is primarily liable to maintain in terms of the repairing clause) consists of air space and internal partitioning surrounded by, but including, certain internal finishes.

Inadequate description

Assuming that the description of the premises leaves something to **2.12** be desired, some assistance may be derived from outwith the terms of the lease principally from two sources:

(1) The overriding implied obligation on the landlord at common law: the common law of Scotland unlike that of England[6] contains such a strong implication that the landlord is liable to keep premises in tenantable condition and wind and watertight, that if a specific part of the building is not included in the description of the premises, the landlord will almost certainly have the obligation to keep it in repair if by not doing so the premises let to the tenant are in less than tenantable condition, or not wind and watertight. Although there is an absence of authority in Scotland on the point, it is thought that this would cover, for instance, a leaking roof which, though not part of the premises, requires to be watertight so that the premises themselves are; or a dangerous common staircase giving access to the premises. For discussion as to when the duty of the landlord to effect repairs arises, see Chapter 4.

(2) Implications from the description of the premises: again there is little authority in Scotland but the following cases may offer some assistance. As ever, these should be treated with extreme caution, first, because each case will depend upon its own facts and the precise wording in the lease and secondly, when the cases are English, because of the fundamentally different underlying common law in Scotland which places so much more by way of implied repairing obligations upon a landlord than does English law.[7] Subject to this caveat, the following cases may be looked at:

Boswell v. Crucible Steel Co[8]: large plate glass windows which were designed to be unopenable were held to be part of the structure of the building concerned and therefore outwith the tenant's

---

[6] See, *e.g. Hart v. Windsor* (1844) 12 M. & W. 68 (no implied duty on the landlord to put premises into repair before letting them); *Gott v. Gandy* (1853) 3 E. & B. 845 (landlord has no implied duty to repair premises during the lease).
[7] *Hart v. Windsor* (1844) 12 M. & W. 68; *Gott v. Gandy* (1853) 3 E. & B. 845.
[8] [1925] 1 K.B. 119.

obligation to repair, which did not extend to structural parts. It is assumed that this decision would apply with even more force to modern curtain walling and the glazing incorporated therein.

Holiday Fellowship v. Viscount Hereford[9]: roofs and main walls of a building were excepted from the tenant's repairing obligation, but it was held that ordinary wooden framed windows did not form part of the main walls and were therefore not covered by the exception.

Twyman v. Charrington[10]: under a sub-lease of the ground and basement floors of a house where the landlord occupied the upper floors and where the description of the premises sub-let was vague, the court held that the sub-tenant, under his obligation to contribute to the cost of repairs to, *inter alia*, "mutual structures", was liable to contribute to the cost of repairs to the roof of the building even though it was not physically adjacent to the premises sub-let. The same approach would be adopted in the case of external walls.

Granada Theatres Ltd v. Freehold Investment (Leytonstone) Ltd[11]: the lease of a cinema provided that "nothing in this clause ... shall render the tenant liable for structural repairs of a substantial nature to the main walls, roof, foundations or main drains of the demised building". A substantial amount of rendering to brickwork had fallen away removing part of the brickwork itself. A substantial number of slates on the roof also had to be replaced. In the Court of Appeal Vaisey J. said:

> "It appears, rather surprisingly, that the expression 'structural repairs' has never been judicially defined, a fact to which attention is drawn in Woodfall on the Landlord and Tenant, 25th Edition, page 770, paragraph 1732, and Counsel in the present case accepted that statement as correct. The writer of the text book submits on the same page that 'structural repairs' are those which involve interference with, or alteration to, the framework of the building, and I would myself say that 'structural repairs' means repairs of, or to, a structure."

Note, however, that the word "structure" can also mean a building or anything erected on land. The last statement should therefore be treated with caution.

---

[9]　[1959] 1 W.L.R. 211.
[10]　[1994] 1 EGLR 243.
[11]　[1959] Ch. 592.

Hastie v. City of Edinburgh District Council[12] ("structure and exterior" of a house under Housing (Scotland) Act 1985): "the structure of a house is that part of it which gives it stability, shape and identity as a house. The essentials seem ... to be foundations, walls and roof... the exterior of a house is the part of the house which lies between what is outside the house and what is inside the house."

Douglas-Scott v. Scorgie[13]: the roof of a block of flats, particularly if a flat roof not physically separated from the ceiling of the top flat, could be part of the structure and exterior of a top floor flat even though it was not expressly contained in the description of the premises.

Camden Hill Towers v. Gardner[14]: a rather specialised case involving the Housing Act 1961 in which the exterior of a flat was held to include only the outside of the particular flat and not the exterior of the whole building.

These last two cases seem fortuitously to reflect the common **2.13** law of tenement in Scotland (see paragraph 2.10), but the Scottish courts are unlikely to apply the common law of tenement to a situation where the landlord owns the whole of a building and merely lets out individual flats. The common law would apply between separate owners of the tenement building (unless, of course, the title deeds provide otherwise), but in a situation where the landlord owns the whole tenement and has failed adequately to describe what has been let (*e.g.* by merely describing the premises as "the southmost first floor flat") the Scottish courts might well prefer to rely upon the underlying common law and find the landlord liable to keep the structure and exterior in tenantable condition and wind and watertight, leaving the tenant liable merely for the interior. The result may well depend upon the extent of the tenant's repairing obligation in the lease: thus if the repairing obligations specifically require the tenant to maintain and repair the interior and exterior of the premises and keep them wind and watertight, the courts might infer that the description includes the exterior in order to give sense to the wording of the lease. The matter has been discussed in a

---

[12] 1981 S.L.T. (Sh.Ct.) 61 and 92.
[13] [1984] 1 W.L.R. 716.
[14] [1977] Q.B. 823.

recent Scottish case[15] in which there was a lease of certain premises at first, second and third floor levels (without much more by way of description), coupled with a specific obligation on the landlord to maintain, *inter alia*, the structure, roof and walls of the building. There was also a list of specific common parts to the maintenance of which the tenant would have to contribute. The list did not include the roof and walls specifically but the last item on the list was: "all other parts of, fixtures and fittings used in connection with and services in the said building ... which are common to the premises and other parts of the said building". Lord President Hope, who delivered the judgment of the Inner House, stated that the common law of tenement did not apply in leases to assist in determining what would or would not be common parts since that matter fell to be regulated by the terms of the lease. In the instant case, however, he held that the roof and exterior walls fell within the last item in the list of common parts (see above) and that the tenant was therefore liable to contribute. Clearly the result in any particular case will depend on the precise terms of the individual lease.

Other specific provisions

2.14 The particular lease may, of course, oblige the tenant to maintain or repair a specific item which may not form part of the premises as defined. Thus a lease may oblige the tenant to clean the glass in the windows, either inside only or both sides, even though on a strict interpretation of the definition of the premises in that particular lease, the windows do not technically form part of the premises. There might be an argument if the windows were described as the "windows of the premises" because technically, the premises would exclude the windows (in this example) but again the courts would probably wish to give effect to the obvious intention of the provision rather than adopt a restrictive legalistic approach.

The repairing clause

2.15 As was pointed out in paragraph 1.1, the common law implies a warranty by the landlord that the premises, at the start of the lease, are fit for the purpose for which they are let.[16] As has already been

---

[15] *Marfield v. Secretary of State for the Environment,* 1996 S.C.L.R. 749.
[16] *Turners Trs. v. Steel* (1900) 2 F. 363.

mentioned,[17] in the case of a lease of premises forming part of a building owned by one landlord but in multiple occupation, this implied warranty extends not only to the premises let but also to the common parts of the building. In that case the landlord failed to recover through the service charge a proportion of the cost of repairing defective tanking in the basement of the building because although the tenant had signed a clause in the lease accepting the premises in their then condition (thus negating the landlord's implied warranty as to their fitness for the purpose) there was no similar clause relating to the common parts. The case is perhaps a little strange since the effect of such an implied warranty in relation to the actual premises let (as opposed to common parts) can, if breached (and not negated by the express terms of the lease), water down an apparently full repairing obligation on a tenant. However, it is difficult to see how it could water down a similar obligation upon a landlord since a landlord can hardly be said to have granted a warranty to himself; in any event the landlord would have a fairly full common law liability to repair common parts regardless of the express provisions of the lease in this case: see paragraph 4.2. What the case was concerned with was not really the landlord's liability to carry out the works but the tenant's liability to reimburse. Be that as it may, regardless of the scope of the repairing obligation, the tenant may be able to pray in aid the landlord's implied warranty.

On the assumption that the landlord has not fallen at the hurdle **2.16** of the warranty of fitness for purpose, the wording of the repairing clause has to be closely examined. Because of the underlying common law position examined in Chapter 1, a "full repairing" clause (*i.e.* one which shifts the whole responsibility of repairing, maintaining and possibly rebuilding or renewing on to the tenant) has to be far more tightly drawn in Scotland than in England, as English law does not tend to imply much by way of repairing liability upon a landlord. Against that background, it will be helpful to examine a fairly typical clause found in modern full repairing and insuring leases in an attempt to interpret the meaning of the various expressions used in the light of the available authorities. It needs to be stressed once again that each case will turn on its own facts and the language used and that, as is often the case, there is

---

[17] *Blackwell v. Farmfoods (Aberdeen) Ltd,* 1991 G.W.D. 4–219.

little authority in Scotland on the matter, thus requiring the courts to seek assistance from English authorities. However, in a recent Scottish case in the Outer House of the Court of Session, the language of a repairing clause was comprehensively examined by Lord Penrose.[18] The clause was contained in two leases, which were in all material respects identical, of parts of the Anderston Cross Centre, Glasgow. The leases dated from 1975 and so the repairing clauses are perhaps not in quite the latest form. They deserve analysis nonetheless. It should also be noted that the leases were "multiple occupancy" leases (see paragraph 2.11) and, therefore, that the structure of the buildings was retained by, and was the responsibility of, the landlord to repair, so that the premises consisted of an "interior" part of the buildings.

2.17   The wording of the repairing clause in the leases in question is contained in a paragraph of one of the schedules to the leases: the obligation as set out in that paragraph can be broken down into the following separate obligations which the tenant undertook, namely:

(1) to accept the premises in their present condition;

(2) to fit them out forthwith for the tenant's business only in accordance with plans and specifications to be submitted in triplicate and previously approved by the landlord in writing;

(3) at its own cost and expense to repair [the premises] and keep [them] in good and substantial condition and repaired and maintained, decorated, paved and cleansed in every respect all to the satisfaction of the landlord;

(4) to replace, renew or rebuild whenever necessary the premises and all additions thereto, and all drains, soil and other pipes, sewers, sanitary and water apparatus, glass, vaults, pavement lights and parts, pertinents and others therein or thereon.

These component obligations will be examined in turn in the succeeding paragraphs.

2.18   *"to accept the premises in their present condition"*: this wording has already been commented upon as removing the implied warranty by the landlord of fitness for the purposes of the tenant's business: see paragraph 1.1, and note that the clause in this instance would not have covered the structural and common parts of the

---

[18] *Taylor Woodrow Property Company Ltd v. Strathclyde Regional Council*, 1996 G.W.D. 7–397.

building — with which, however, the case was not principally concerned.

"to fit them out forthwith for the tenant's business": wording **2.19** such as this is dealt with in paragraph 3.6 dealing with alterations and the obligation to hand back the premises at the term of a lease in a particular condition.

"at its own cost and expense to repair":

(1) The clause from the leases in question contains the phrase **2.20** "all to the satisfaction of the landlord" which is not very commonly found since the word "satisfaction" is almost always qualified by the word "reasonable". The case contained a great deal of discussion as to whether any, and if so what, qualification should be implied of what might appear to be an entirely subjective test. Several English and Scottish authorities were referred to,[19] but Lord Penrose concluded: "The question for enquiry therefore is whether in stipulating for repair of any item the landlords acted reasonably in defining the scope of the work required, having regard *inter alia* to their own interests as owners of the building, and the fact that the position of the obligant is that of tenant under a lease of the premises".

(2) Lord Penrose considered that there was a distinction to be drawn between an obligation "to repair" and an obligation "to keep in good and substantial condition and in repair" and quoted with approval an English case where Lindsay J. concluded that "all that is needed, in general terms, to trigger a need for activity under an obligation to keep in (and put into) a given condition is that the subject matter is out of that condition".[20] Lord Penrose therefore concluded that there was no need for any *specific* element of disrepair to be identified as a precondition of work under an obligation "to keep in good and substantial condition and repair" being required. As an illustration of the distinction, Lord Penrose referred to another English case where the court held that, under a

---

[19] See, *e.g. Associated Provincial Picture Houses Ltd v. Wednesbury Corp.* [1948] 1 K.B. 223, where the test in the case of exercise of administrative power was held to be whether any reasonable decision maker acting reasonably in the circumstances could have arrived at the decision in question; *Gordon District Council v. Wimpey Homes Holdings Ltd,* 1989 S.L.T. 141 where, in a commercial contract between purchaser and seller, a test similar to that adopted by Lord Penrose in *Taylor Woodrow* was applied.

[20] *Credit Suisse v. Beegas Nominees Ltd (No. 1)* [1994] 11 EG 151.

simple obligation to repair (which did not include the words "keep in repair"), the tenant did not need to install asphalt tanking in a basement which, by virtue of its construction, let in water. No damage to the building had been caused by the ingress of water and therefore there was no damage to repair.[21] Furthermore, a contractual obligation "to keep in repair" is broken as soon as the defect becomes evident[22] and this may impose immediate liability upon the party under the obligation (*e.g.* for damages if, for instance, a landlord whose tenant has the obligation to keep in repair, loses money on the disposal of his interest as a result of the disrepair — even if the defect is remedied without undue delay). If the obligation were simply to repair, a reasonable time would be allowed to carry out the repair in question. But note that where the repairing obligation rests with the landlord and relates to parts of the building which are let to and occupied by the tenant, even an obligation to keep in repair is not breached until the defect is brought to his attention and he is afforded a reasonable time to remedy it (see paragraph 1.2).

(3) Subject to the caveat in sub-paragraph 7, an obligation "to repair" will include the obligation to renew component parts of a building. There clearly comes a point where, in order to repair, so much renewal of component parts is involved as to amount to virtual renewal of the building. In *Lurcott v. Wakely and Wheeler,*[23] the tenant was obliged to reimburse the landlord the cost of demolishing a flank wall which was dangerous, and rebuilding a new wall in accordance with the then current statutory requirements. On the other hand, the tenant who had a general obligation to repair, was, in another English case, held not liable to pay the cost of demolishing and rebuilding an old house where all the walls were dangerous and bulging because of insufficient foundations.[24] In the *Taylor Woodrow* case, Lord Penrose, however, rejected an argument mounted on behalf of the tenant, that one had to look at the specific component in question (*e.g.* a roof) in order to determine whether what was being requested was repair or renewal. The

---

[21] *Post Office v. Aquarius Properties Ltd* [1987] 1 EGLR 40, following *Quick v. Taff-Ely Borough Council* [1986] Q.B. 809.

[22] *British Telecommunications plc v. Sun Life Assurance Society plc* [1995] 3 W.L.R. 622, approved by Lord Penrose in *Taylor Woodrow*.

[23] [1911] 1 K.B. 905 quoted with approval by Lord Penrose in *Taylor Woodrow*.

[24] *Lister v. Lane & Nesham* [1893] 2 Q.B. 212; *Penbery v. Lamdin* [1940] 2 All E.R. 434.

correct view was to look at the building as a whole. What might be considered to be renewal as regards the roof, would only amount to repair as regards the building as a whole.

(4) Under a simple obligation to repair, a tenant does not have to hand back a different thing from that which was let[25] or to improve the premises. Clearly, in order to carry out repair, renewal or improvement of component parts of the premises may be required since, for instance, new slates are likely to be an improvement upon old slates. Looked at in the context of the building as a whole, this would merely be regarded as subordinate renewal falling within the obligation to repair.[26] By contrast, in *Brew Brothers Ltd v. Ross Snax Ltd,*[27] the tenant avoided liability for rebuilding a dangerous flank wall by showing that its replacement would cost almost as much as building a new building. This decision (which was a majority decision of the Court of Appeal in England, thus showing that it was a difficult and borderline case) appears to have been based upon relative costs (repair as against complete renewal) rather than whether the wall was a component part of the whole building (which it doubtless was) and rests somewhat uneasily with the *Lurcott* case.[28] It also appears to run counter to the decision in *Elite Investments Ltd v. T.I. Bainbridge Silencers Ltd*[29] where the tenant, again under a simple obligation to repair, was held liable for the cost of replacing a whole roof, even though the cost was almost as much as the value of the building. The English courts tend to arrive at different decisions depending upon whether the property let was an old building at the commencement of the lease and depending upon the duration of the lease itself, favouring a more lenient interpretation where the building is old at commencement and where the lease is short. As ever, there is little authority as to whether these distinctions would be made in Scotland and the cases, if they show anything, show the difficulty the English courts have had in reaching decisions in what might be described as "difficult" cases. As already mentioned, previous cases on apparently similar facts can be helpful but cannot always be implicitly relied upon, especially if not Scottish cases. Again the caveat set out in sub-paragraph 7 should always be borne in mind.

---

[25] *Lister v. Lane & Nesham, supra; Penbery v. Lamdin, supra.*
[26] *Lurcott v. Wakely and Wheeler* [1911] 1 K.B. 905.
[27] [1970] 1 Q.B. 612.
[28] *Lurcott v. Wakely and Wheeler, supra.*
[29] [1986] 2 EGLR 43.

(5) In England, a simple obligation "to repair" is deemed to include an obligation "to put into repair", even if the premises are let in a state of disrepair.[30] There is little authority on this point in Scotland although the very recent case of *Lowe v. Quayle Munro Ltd*[31] may throw some light upon the point. In that case the repairing obligation upon the tenant was:

> "To accept the leased subjects in their present condition and at their own cost and expense to repair and keep in good and substantial repair and maintained ... in every respect all to the satisfaction of the Landlords and to replace or renew or rebuild whenever necessary the leased subjects and all additions thereto ... and parts, pertinents and others therein and thereon all to the satisfaction of the Landlords and that regardless of the age or state of dilapidation of the buildings or others for the time being comprised in the leased subjects and irrespective of any latent or inherent defects therein."

Counsel for both parties agreed that the opening words of the clause displaced the landlord's implied warranty as to condition at the commencement of the lease but they were in dispute as to whether there was a bench mark condition as at the date of commencement of the lease to which the obligation to "repair and keep in good and substantial repair and maintained" related. Counsel for the defenders argued that the starting point was "present condition" and that unless there was a failure to maintain that condition, there was no trigger for the obligation to repair. Counsel for the pursuer argued that the state of the premises at the date of entry did not qualify the repairing obligation which was a very wide one. The trigger was simply the identification of a need for repair or other work, however it had arisen. The initial acceptance of the premises on the terms of the clause supported that view. Lord Penrose concluded that the key to the interpretation of the clause lay in the application of the disregard of inherent defects to each aspect of the clause and he construed the clause as if it had commenced:

> "To accept the leased subjects in their present condition... and that regardless of the age or state of dilapidation of the buildings or others for the time being comprised in the leased subjects and irrespective of any latent or inherent defects therein."

---

[30] *Proudfoot v. Hart* (1890) 25 Q.B.D. 42, *per* Lord Esher at p. 50.
[31] 1997 G.W.D. 10–438.

He then went on to say that the same words of disregard then qualified each and every obligation of repair or renewal from a clear bench mark at the date of entry. The inference to be drawn from Lord Penrose's judgment is that if the words of disregard to which Lord Penrose referred had not been included, he might have had difficulty in finding the tenant liable to *put* the premises into good repair. However, it seems to the author that the existence of the words "to keep in good and substantial repair" would have assisted in applying a bench mark conditon in any event — even if the premises had not been in that condition at the start of the lease. Whether or not that is so, it may be safer from the perspective of the landlord for the tenant's obligation to include words such as "to accept the premises as in good, substantial and tenantable condition and fit for the purpose for which they are let", thus making the position crystal clear. Again, the caveat set out at sub-paragraph 7 should always be borne in mind.

(6) A simple obligation "to repair" may include an obligation to effect a design improvement, if building regulations so require, provided that repair is merely the renewal or replacement of component parts of the building. In *Ravenseft Property Ltd v. Davstone (Holdings) Ltd*[32] the tenant was obliged to insert expansion joints when repairing (which effectively involved replacing) brick cladding which had bulged dangerously as a result of their omission from the original design. Again the caveat set out at sub-paragraph 7 should always be borne in mind.

(7) The foregoing paragraphs as to the interpretation of "repair" must be read subject to the overriding caveat that, in Scotland, the obligation on a tenant to repair will not, without more express wording, oblige the tenant to carry out what are known as "extraordinary repairs".[33] Such repairs include those becoming necessary as a result of inevitable decay caused by lapse of time or wear and tear. It would certainly not oblige a tenant to remedy latent or structural defects. Accordingly, modern full repairing leases in Scotland invariably include wording to the effect that the tenant's obligation to repair will apply "irrespective of the cause of damage necessitating such repair". Wording such as this has been held effective in fixing the tenant with an obligation to carry out repairs to a television mast even where it became damaged as a result of

---

[32] [1980] Q.B. 12.
[33] *Turners Trs. v. Steel* (1900) 2 F. 363; *Johnstone v. Hugham* (1894) 21 R. 777.

an inherent design defect.[34] As will be seen in Chapter 4 this limitation on the tenant's liability to repair does not apply to a similarly phrased obligation upon a landlord.[35]

(8) Once more subject to the caveat referred to in sub-paragraph 7, the following cases may be helpful in establishing the standard of repair or in determining the meaning of certain other phrases often found in repairing clauses. Whilst they may be helpful, they must be regarded as no more than that since, apart from differences in the underlying common law where the cases quoted are English, each case will to a greater or lesser extent turn on its own facts and depend upon the particular provisions in the lease concerned.

2.21 *Proudfoot v. Hart*[36] (definition of "tenantable repair"):

> "good tenantable repair is such repair as, having regard to the age, character and locality of the house, would make it reasonably fit for the occupation of a reasonably minded tenant of the class who would be likely to take it. The age of the house must be taken into account, because nobody could reasonably expect that a house two hundred years old should be in the same condition of repair as a house lately built; the character of the house must be taken into account, because the same class of repairs as would be necessary to a palace would be wholly unnecessary to a cottage; and the locality of the house must be taken into account, because the state of repair necessary for a house in Grosvenor Square would be wholly different to the state of repair necessary for a house in Spitalfields. The house need not be put into the same condition as when the tenant took it; it need not be put into perfect repair; it need only be put into such a state of repair as renders it reasonably fit for the occupation of a reasonably minded tenant of the class who would be likely to take it."

Anstruther-Gough-Calthorpe v. McOscar[37]: the test formulated in *Proudfoot v. Hart* was considered in detail in this case and was approved even although the obligation in question did not include the word "tenantable". It is therefore probable in England that the same test (*i.e.* the *Proudfoot v. Hart* test) would be applied in relation to a simple obligation to keep in repair. However, in the *McOscar* case the court also stated that the hypothetical class of tenants who

---

[34] *Thorn EMI Ltd v. Taylor Woodrow Industrial Estates Ltd,* Court of Session, October 1982, unreported.

[35] *House of Fraser plc v. Prudential Assurance Co Ltd,* 1994 S.L.T. 416.

[36] (1890) 25 Q.B.D. 42.

[37] [1924] 1 K.B. 716.

would be likely to take the property on lease (referred to in the *Proudfoot* case) must be the same class of tenants who would have taken the lease at its commencement and not the class who might take it at termination of the lease, if because of a deterioration in the neighbourhood (or perhaps an improvement) the class at termination is different.

Plough Investments Ltd v. Manchester City Council[38]: in relation to cracks in the curtain walling of a steel framed building put up in the twenties, Scott J. said:

> "nor, in my opinion, would the obligation to repair include the removal and replacement of every cracked brick or block, no matter how small the cracks. There were cracks when the leases were granted. A building of this sort, over sixty years old, is bound, in my view to have some cracks in the bricks or blocks."

Haskell v. Marlow[39] (meaning of reasonable wear and tear):

> "The meaning is that the tenant is bound to keep the house in good repair and condition, but is not liable for what is due to reasonable wear and tear. That is to say, his obligation to keep in good repair is subject to that exception. If any want of repair is alleged and proved in fact, it lies on the tenant to show that comes within the exception. Reasonable wear and tear means the reasonable use of the house by the tenant and the ordinary operation of natural forces."

Regis Property Co. Ltd v. Dudley[40] (consequential damage in relation to exclusion of fair wear and tear). Lord Denning in the House of Lords stated:

> "I have never understood that in an ordinary house a 'fair wear and tear' exception reduced the burden of repairs to practically nothing at all. It exempts a tenant from liability for repairs that are decorative and for remedying parts that wear out or come adrift in the course of reasonable use, but it does not exempt him from anything else. If further damage is likely to flow from the wear and tear, he must do such repairs as are necessary to stop that further damage. If a slate falls off through wear and tear and in consequence the roof is likely to let through water, the tenant is not responsible for the slate coming off but he ought to put in another one to prevent further damage."

---

[38] [1989] 1 EGLR 244.
[39] [1928] 2 K.B. 45.
[40] [1959] A.C. 370.

This clearly limits the scope of a "fair wear and tear" exception in that sort of case in England.

Granada Theatres Ltd v. Freehold Investments (Leytonstone) Ltd[41] (Structural repairs): "Those which involve interference with, or alteration to, the framework of the building"; "repairs of or to a structure." See paragraph 2.12.

Credit Suisse v. Beegas Nominees Ltd[42] ("repair" as opposed to "keep in good and substantial condition and repair"): the defects concerned in this case were seals around double glazed window units inserted into aluminium panels each of which interlocked horizontally and vertically with its neighbours. The point was that there was nothing particularly in a state of disrepair which required to be repaired. Accordingly a simple obligation "to repair" would not have obliged the landlord (in this case it was the landlord's repairing obligation which was being looked at) to do anything. However, the obligation was "to maintain, repair, amend, renew, cleanse, repaint and redecorate and *otherwise keep in good and tenantable condition*" (author's italics). Lindsay J. held that whilst the simple obligation to repair would not oblige the landlord to take action the words in italics did so because the premises were clearly *not* in good and tenantable condition.

2.22   "*to replace, renew or rebuild whenever necessary*": these words impose an obligation well beyond ordinary "repair" and would include the obligation completely to rebuild in appropriate cases. In an English case[43] it was held that the increased burden of this obligation, over and above the simple obligation to repair, entitled the tenant to a 27.5 per cent discount on the rent which would otherwise have been fixed at review. Even if a Scottish lease did not include the words "irrespective of the cause of damage necessitating such repair" as a rider to the tenant's obligation to repair (see paragraph 2.20, sub-paragraph 7), the courts in Scotland might find it difficult not to give effect to words such as "replace, renew or rebuild wherever necessary". The courts will endeavour to give meaning to all the relevant words used in the particular

---

[41] [1959] Ch. 592.
[42] [1991] 4 All E.R. 803.
[43] *Norwich Union Life Insurance Society v. British Railways Board* [1987] 2 EGLR 137.

clause.[44] So, including wording such as "to replace, renew or rebuild whenever necessary" may well be sufficient to compensate for the omission of the repair rider ("irrespective of the cause of damage") in appropriate cases. For the draughtsman on behalf of the landlord, it would be safer to include the rider until a definite decision that it is unnecessary has been given by a Scottish court!

Other relevant clauses

Whilst the initial part of a repairing obligation upon a tenant in a **2.23** lease may well appear to be all embracing, the tenant's adviser should always be aware that there may be a qualification in a later part of the clause, or even in a separate clause, to the effect that, despite the repairing obligation (and possibly other obligations, such as compliance with statute or title deeds[45]), the tenant does not have to do any work which would render the premises in any condition better than that disclosed in what is known as a "schedule of condition"; typically this will consist of a schedule to the lease containing a photographic record of the condition of the premises at the commencement of the lease, usually accompanied by a brief description of that condition.

Apart from the repairing clause, the tenant may have liability to carry out work by virtue of the provisions of other clauses in the lease. These are dealt with in Chapter 3.

---

[44] *Anstruther-Gough-Calthorpe v. McOscar* [1924] 1 K.B. 716.
[45] See Chap. 3.

CHAPTER 3

PROVISIONS (OTHER THAN THE REPAIRING CLAUSE) OF THE LEASE OR CONTRACT

Quite apart from the repairing clause proper, there are several other **3.1** provisions in most commercial leases which have an impact on work which the tenant may have to do either during, but more especially at the termination of, the lease. Principal amongst these are provisions relating to decoration, fittings and fixtures, alterations and compliance with statutory and title provisions.

Decoration

Single occupancy leases normally oblige the tenant to decorate the **3.2** exterior and interior of the premises at fixed intervals, the favoured frequency currently being three yearly for external work and five yearly for internal work. Multiple occupancy leases normally oblige the tenant to carry out internal decoration only (normally at five yearly intervals) with the landlord normally being obliged to carry out external decoration (sometimes at specified intervals), the tenants in the building being responsible between them through a service charge for the total costs incurred by the landlord in doing so. The matter of contribution to service charges is dealt with in more detail in Chapter 4. It should be noted that even if the tenant has complied with his obligation to decorate at specified intervals, if the decorative condition of the premises falls outwith the "good and tenantable" state in which (if it does so) the repairing clause obliges the tenant to keep it, this will nonetheless constitute a breach of the tenant's obligations under that repairing clause. Conversely, notwithstanding that the premises may be in good and tenantable condition, an obligation to decorate in specific years is probably an absolute obligation.[1] As to the landlord's remedies, see Chapter 5. A typical decoration clause in modern commercial leases may also require the tenant to clean the external stonework at fixed

---

[1] *Gemmell v. Goldsworthy* [1942] S.A.S.R. 55 (an Australian case).

intervals but whilst that specific obligation may well be enforced in its terms by the courts, it would seem unlikely that it would be covered by the obligations contained in a general repairing clause.

Landlord's and tenant's fixtures

3.3 The clause defining the premises often includes items such as fitted carpets specifically as part of the premises and thus included in all obligations of the tenant which relate to the premises as defined. In the absence of any precise definition, the law lays down certain tests as to whether an item is a fixture (which would be part of the heritable property or premises and thus, subject to comments in paragraph 3.4 on tenant's or trade fixtures, covered by the tenant's obligations relating to the premises), or merely moveable and thus not part of the premises nor covered by the relevant repairing obligations. The tests are considered in *Scottish Discount Co. Ltd v. Blin.*[2] Lord President Emslie stated in that case that whilst cases relating to rating and valuation law, which applies to "lands and heritages", might be helpful, they do not attempt to distinguish property rights as between landlord and tenant and are therefore to be treated with caution in any context other than valuation. The proper tests to determine whether an item is or is not a heritable fixture include:

(1) The fact of attachment and the degree of attachment — though these are not to be seen as decisive without consideration of other factors.

(2) Whether the item can be removed without the destruction of the item itself or of the soil or building to which it is attached.

(3) Whether the attachment is of a permanent or *quasi*-permanent character.

(4) Whether the building to which it was attached was specially adapted for its use.

(5) How far the use or enjoyment of the soil or building would be affected by its removal.

(6) The intention of the party attaching it as discoverable from the nature of the article and the building and the manner in which it is affixed and not from extrinsic evidence as to what was in the mind of the party who affixed it.

---

[2] 1985 S.C. 216, which was quoted with approval in the *Taylor Woodrow* case analysed in Chap. 2.

However, even if it is established that the item concerned is a **3.4**
fixture forming part of the premises,[3] it may still be either a
landlord's fixture or a tenant's fixture. Landlord's fixtures will
include items affixed to the premises by the landlord (or a previous
tenant or occupier) and let as part of the original lease to the current
tenant and those affixed by the landlord (either with the tenant's
agreement or in terms of the lease) during the lease as well as those
affixed by the tenant unless they are such as he is entitled to remove
at the end of the lease in which case they are called tenant's or
trade fixtures. An item which the tenant has introduced on to the
premises for the purposes of his trade or manufacture will normally
be regarded as a tenant's fixture which he is entitled to remove
unless (1) the lease otherwise provides or (2) the removal of the
item would cause irreparable injury to the premises.[4]

If the item concerned is found, applying those tests, to be a **3.5**
tenant's or trade fixture, then unless the lease otherwise provides
(or the item was affixed in breach of the provisions of the lease,
e.g. as to alterations) the tenant will be entitled, but not obliged, to
remove it at the termination of the lease.[5] During the course of the
lease, tenant's fixtures will be part of the premises and subject to
the repairing obligations that relate to them, though with this
difference, that the tenant can remove the fixtures concerned (unless
of course the lease provides otherwise) and so escape the repairing
obligation altogether. At termination of the lease, if they are not
removed by the tenant, they will be subject to the same repairing
obligations as relate to the premises themselves. If removed, the
tenant will be responsible for making good damage caused to the
premises by their removal.[6]

---

[3] For a useful guide to what are likely to be removable fittings on the one hand
and non-removable fixtures on the other, see *Botham v. TSB Bank plc* [1996]
EGCS 149, a case which concerned ordinary household items such as kitchen
units, fitted carpets, etc., and a dispute between a repossesing bank and the
mortgagor of the house.

[4] *Smith v. City Petroleum Co. Ltd* [1940] 1 All E.R. 260. For a fuller discussion
of fixtures, see Gordon, *Scottish Land Law* (1989), Chap. 5.

[5] *Taylor Woodrow Property Company Ltd v. Strathclyde Regional Council,* 1996
G.W.D. 7–397.

[6] *ibid.*

Alterations and improvements

3.6 Most leases contain specific clauses restricting the tenant's right to
make alterations or improvements to the premises. In the absence
of any specific provision the tenant of commercial property can
normally make only very minor alterations to the premises without
the consent of his landlord because of the common law rule against
"inversion of possession" (*i.e.* treating the premises in a way which
is outwith the scope of the lease).[7] If alterations have been made in
breach of the lease or the common law, the landlord can, of course,
require their removal and the reinstatement of the premises. Most
leases permit certain types of alteration provided the landlord's
prior written consent is obtained and this consent is usually
incorporated in a licence for works agreement between the parties.
This will typically provide for the tenant, if so required by the
landlord, to restore the premises to their pre-alteration condition at
the end of the lease and make good all damage caused by such
restoration. It will also normally provide that all obligations in the
lease, including the repairing obligations, are to apply to the post-
alteration premises just as they applied to the pre-alteration
premises. Even if no such provisions were made, the alteration
concerned will become part of the premises for the purposes of the
lease if it is so attached as to become a fixture (see paragraph 3.3)
or if, more obviously, it becomes part of the "structure" of the
premises proper. In the case of an alteration becoming a fixture,
the distinction between the landlord's and tenant's fixtures will
still fall to be applied, subject always to any specific provision in
the lease or licence for works. It should be noted that there is no
statutory or common law requirement in Scotland, in contrast to
the position in England,[8] requiring a landlord to pay his tenant
compensation for improvements at the end of a lease, except in the
case of agricultural leases (see Chapter 7).

Compliance with statutory and title requirements

3.7 Commercial leases almost invariably contain a clause binding the
tenant to comply with statutory notices and orders whether served

---

[7] Paton and Cameron, *The Law of Landlord and Tenant in Scotland,* p. 137.

[8] See, *e.g.* Landlord and Tenant Act 1927, which permits a business tenant in
certain circumstances to obtain compensation for improvements on quitting
the premises.

upon the landlord or the tenant. Although these will be construed as applying to the premises or their use, a widely drawn statutory compliance clause could expand the obligations contained in a loosely drawn repairing clause. The obligation to comply with fire and building control regulations would, for instance, result in the need for considerable work to, and even improvement of, the premises, if a new fire escape or fire resistant doors or partitions had to be installed as a result of the service of an appropriate notice. The tenant, to some extent, can control the application of some types of statutory requirements by the manner in which he uses the premises, *e.g.* how many staff are employed and where, but he may in some circumstances have no such control. Often, the statutory provisions contain sections which apportion the cost of such works between those who incur the expense and other parties[9] requiring the court to make such apportionment as it considers just and equitable in the circumstances, regard being had to the terms of any contract between the parties.

Again there is often a clause requiring the tenant to comply with **3.8** the terms of the landlord's title deeds and pay all sums which may become due by the landlord thereunder. Clearly a clause such as this will require the tenant's adviser to check the relevant provisions in the title deeds. An obligation contained in the landlord's title to, say, a flat in a tenement building, to maintain it in good order and repair and/or to contribute to the cost of repairs to common parts of the tenement might assist the landlord in a situation where the repairing clause itself is deficient in some way.

---

[9] *e.g.* Factories Act 1961, s. 170; Fire Precautions Act 1971, s. 28(2).

CHAPTER 4

LANDLORD'S OBLIGATION TO REPAIR AND SERVICE CHARGES

As has been seen in Chapter 1, a landlord at common law, subject **4.1** of course to any express terms of a lease to the contrary, impliedly warrants the fitness of the premises for the purpose for which they are let and is impliedly obliged to maintain them in a tenantable condition and wind and watertight. The landlord's obligation in this situation only arises where he has been given notice of the defect concerned. In other words, the landlord does not have to inspect the premises constantly or manage them so as to ensure that no defect does occur.[1] This, however, is only the case where one is dealing with a single occupancy lease (*i.e.* where the whole premises are let to the tenant) and not where the landlord's obligation to keep in repair relates to parts of a building in multiple occupation which are not let and which remain effectively in the landlord's control. In that situation the landlord is liable to ensure that those parts remain in good repair and his liability to the tenant for damages (if any are suffered) will arise as soon as the defect occurs and regardless of whether the landlord has or has not received notice from the tenant or has or has not carried out the remedial work without delay.[2]

In contrast to an obligation imposed upon a tenant to repair, an **4.2** obligation upon a landlord to repair will be construed, even without the addition of words such as "irrespective of the cause of damage necessitating such repair", as including the obligation to carry out extraordinary repairs necessitated by lapse of time or natural decay or inherent defect. This will apply even where the common law

---

[1] *Wolfson v. Forrester,* 1910 S.C. 675.
[2] *British Telecommunications plc v. Sun Life Assurance Society plc* [1995] 3 W.L.R. 622 cited with approval by Lord Penrose in the *Taylor Woodrow* case analysed in Chap. 2.

implied obligation is set forth as an express contractual obligation upon the landlord without the addition of the words quoted above.[3]

Service charges

4.3 Although a full examination of service charges is outwith the scope of this work, one or two points which impact on the subject of dilapidations may be worthy of note:

(1) Unless the lease stipulates to the contrary, it is likely that a landlord, in carrying out an obligation to repair for which he is entitled to charge the stipulated proportion of the costs incurred in doing so to the tenant, must carry out the work in a "fair and reasonable" manner. In other words, he cannot throw caution to the wind and carry out the work in a ludicrously costly fashion or to a ludicrously high standard. If he does so, he may only be able to recover the costs which he would have incurred in carrying out the works to a standard which the court considers "fair and reasonable".

This matter has very recently come before the Court of Session in *Lowe v. Quayle Munro Ltd*[4] where the pursuer was seeking, amongst other things, to recover a percentage of costs in relation to expenditure incurred by her in respect of common subjects; the relevant part of the clause states:

> "To pay and reimburse to the Landlords on demand Forty *per centum* of the costs properly incurred by the Landlords in maintaining, repairing and where necessary renewing the exterior and structure of the building Number Forty one Charlotte Square".

---

[3] *House of Fraser plc v. Prudential Assurance Co. Ltd,* 1994 S.L.T. 416.

[4] 1997 G.W.D. 10–438. This case appears to support the view of the English courts as stated in *Finchbourne v. Rodrigues* [1976] 3 All E.R. 581 which was approved (although not strictly relevant to the case in point) in *W.W. Promotions (Scotland) Ltd v. De Marco,* 1988 S.L.T. (Sh.Ct.) 43. However there is a new line of authority in England, relating specifically to reimbursement of insurance premiums paid by a landlord and recoverable from his tenant, that there is no implication of reasonableness in choosing an insurer: see *Havenridge v. Boston Dyers Ltd* [1994] 2 EGLR 73 (where the word "properly" was used and was held to amount to much the same thing as "reasonably") and *Berrycroft Management Co. Ltd v. Sinclair Gardens Investments (Kensington) Ltd* [1996] EGCS 143 where there was no term "properly" or "reasonably" specified — and none was implied, thus leaving the tenant to pay an insurance premium which had virtually doubled on a change of insurer by the landlord.

Counsel for the pursuer argued that "properly" did not imply "reasonably" and that provided the expenditure was properly incurred, the pursuer did not need to be reasonable. Lord Penrose considered that "properly" could be interpreted to mean "reasonably" and that even if it could not be so interpreted, there would be no conflict between a contractual stipulation to act "properly" and an implied term obliging the pursuer to act "reasonably". Lord Penrose continued by stating that in *Taylor Woodrow*[5] he had followed the view of Lord Clyde in *Rockliffe Estates plc v. Co-operative Wholesale Society Ltd*[6] that:

"Each party must have intended that the other would act reasonably and I do not consider that it could have been the intention that the purchasers would be entitled to act arbitrarily or unreasonably."

Lord Penrose could see no reason why that comment was not also appropriate to the case before him.

(2) If as is often provided in service charge clauses, the tenant's obligation is to reimburse a stipulated proportion of costs incurred by the landlord in carrying out repairs, then the costs will have to have been *incurred* prior to the termination of the lease in order to permit the landlord to effect the recovery from the tenant.[7]

(3) It has been held in England (and there seems no good reason why the decision should not be followed in Scotland) that whilst a landlord can normally recover through the service charge for professional fees reasonably incurred in relation to advice as to the method of carrying out proposed repairs (to the cost of which the tenant is liable to contribute), he cannot recover fees which relate to schemes or proposals which are more grandiose than that. The case concerned is *Holding & Management Ltd v. Property Holding & Investment Trust plc,*[8] in which a scheme of works which involved removal of the entire brickwork skin of a building was held to go beyond repair (to the costs of which the tenant would have been liable to contribute) and therefore that the tenant was not obliged to pay the professional costs incurred by the landlord in relation to that scheme.

---

[5] *Taylor Woodrow Property Company Ltd v. Strathclyde Regional Council,* 1996 G.W.D. 7–397.

[6] 1994 S.L.T. 592.

[7] *Freehold Equity Trust Ltd v. BL plc* [1987] 283 EG 563, where the court held that the word "incurred" was synonymous with "expended" or "become payable"; so, even if work has been instructed by the landlord, unless bills have become due for payment, the landlord will not be entitled to recover.

[8] [1990] 1 EGLR 65.

CHAPTER 5

LANDLORDS' AND TENANTS' REMEDIES

Introduction

This chapter deals with the remedies under commercial leases; any **5.1** specialities under residential or agricultural leases are dealt with in Chapters 6 and 7. A landlord has a range of remedies for breach by a tenant of his repairing obligation both during and at the end of the lease. A tenant's remedies for breach by the landlord of his repairing obligations usually arise during the lease.

Landlord's remedies

The landlord's remedies depend upon whether they require to be **5.2** exercised during or at the end of the lease. The following remedies are available to the landlord during the currency of the lease:

(1) He may serve a schedule of dilapidations upon the tenant, calling for the tenant to carry out specific works to the premises.

(2) If the tenant fails to comply with the schedule of dilapidations or notice, he may apply to the court for a decree of specific implement, *i.e.* a decree ordaining the tenant to carry out the works concerned in terms of the lease.

(3) If the tenant fails to comply with the schedule of dilapidations or notice he may, provided the lease gives him the power to do so (and most modern commercial leases do so), enter the premises, carry out the works required and then bill the tenant for the costs plus, again if the lease so provides, interest and professional fees.

(4) If the tenant fails to comply with his obligations to repair (or with a schedule of dilapidations or notice, if served) and the landlord has suffered loss, the landlord may sue the tenant for damages.

(5) If the tenant fails to comply with the schedule of dilapidations or notice, he may seek to irritate or forfeit (in other words terminate) the lease.

It should be noted in passing that a landlord may serve a schedule of dilapidations during a lease for reasons quite unrelated to any desire he may have that the works should actually be carried out. Service of a schedule can have a tactical use to enforce compliance by a tenant with quite a different obligation or to force a tenant to reach a compromise agreement on some other disputed aspect arising under the lease. A tenant might, for instance, be persuaded to accept a rent review settlement more favourable to the landlord if the landlord, having served a schedule of dilapidations, then offers to withdraw or modify it in return for a more favourable settlement on the rent review issue. It could also be used as an excuse by a landlord for delaying the grant of consent to an assignation or to a change of use which the landlord might otherwise have to grant but which he would prefer not to grant. For, on the basis of the principle of mutuality of contract, a landlord does not have to perform his obligations if the tenant is in breach of his; and the fact that there is an outstanding schedule of dilapidations may be a simple way for the landlord to establish that the tenant is in breach of his repairing obligations.

5.3 The following remedies are available to a landlord at the termination of a lease, should the tenant have failed to comply with his repairing obligations:

(1) He may again serve a schedule of dilapidations, although if one was served shortly before the lease expired, he is unlikely to do so again. As will be seen, the reason for doing so is not so much to require the tenant to carry out the works as to record the defects and want of repair in detail so that the schedule can be used both as a record of the condition of the premises at termination and as the basis for negotiating settlement of a claim for a financial settlement from the tenant in lieu of his carrying out the works.

(2) He may sue the tenant for damages for breach of contract, whether or not any schedule of dilapidations or notice was ever served.

These and the remedies available for the landlord during a lease will now be examined in more detail.

Service of Schedule of Dilapidations

5.4 This is otherwise known as a "Notice of Wants of Repair" but the English "Schedule of Dilapidations" is almost always used. A notice does not require to take any specific form and in simple cases could merely list a few defects which the landlord requires to be put right. Such schedules, when served during a lease, are often served at or about the time when the tenant seeks consent to assign or sub-let — since these events often give the landlord a lever to have the works done as a condition of giving consent (assuming landlord's consent is required in terms of the lease, as is most likely). Before serving a schedule of dilapidations, the landlord's agent should carefully check the terms of the lease and ancillary documents (see Chapter 2) to ensure, first, that the works called for fall within the scope of the tenant's obligations and, secondly, that the schedule (which is after all a written notice) is properly and correctly served upon the tenant in terms of the clause, if there is one, relating to the service of notices. Whilst this is sound advice at all times, it has been held that, provided the tenant has actually received the notice and it was served in time, it does not matter that it was not served strictly in accordance with its terms.[1]

5.5 A schedule of dilapidations may also be served at or after the expiry of a lease. Although there is no authority on the point in Scotland it is thought that a landlord will not be able to obtain the remedy of specific implement (see paragraph 5.6) after the expiry of the lease: in other words, that the landlord will be unable to obtain a court decree ordaining the tenant to go back into the premises *after* the expiry of the lease to carry out the works unless of course the lease provides for this — which would be most unusual. The schedule should however be precise enough, particularly if served *during* the lease, both to enable the court to ordain specific implement by the tenant, should that be a possible remedy, and to permit the court to assess damages should it not.

Specific implement

5.6 As a general rule, Scots law allows the injured party, where a contractual obligation other than for the payment of money has not been performed,

---

[1] *Blythswood Investments (Scotland) Ltd v. Clydesdale Electrical Stores Ltd (In Receivership) and the Joint Receivers thereof,* 1995 S.L.T. 150. The case was decided on the basis of the type of "notice" clause most commonly found in commercial leases. The typical clause states that if the notice is served in the prescribed manner, it will be deemed to have been properly served. It does not go on to say that if served in any other manner it will be deemed not to have been served — though there is no reason why a lease should not provide for that in specific terms. *Capital Landholdings Ltd v. Secretary of State for the Environment,* 1996 S.L.T. 1379 where it was held that the requirement that "any notice to the [Landlord] still be sent to its registered office" was mandatory.

the remedy of specific implement: in other words, the court will generally require the party in breach to do what he contracted to do. Where the obligation, as in the case of an obligation to repair, is a positive obligation, the court decree of specific implement is known as a decree *ad factum praestandum, i.e.* a decree to carry out an act. Although this is an equitable remedy and the court may refuse it if not satisfied it is fair and reasonable in all the circumstances to grant it, the court, as a general rule, will, where a party is in breach of an obligation to do something, grant the injured party a decree *ad factum praestandum* as of right.[2] There are various exceptions to this rule:

(1) Where it would cause exceptional hardship.[3]

(2) Where the obligation is merely to pay a sum of money, the courts will not grant the decree since the penalty for failing to obey a decree *ad factum praestandum* may be imprisonment for an individual as such failure is treated as contempt of court; where the failure is by a company, then a fine will be imposed. The courts in such a case will simply allow the creditor to sue for debt and enforce any decree obtained, enabling the creditor to effect the usual civil remedy of diligence (*e.g.* arrestment of the debtor's bank account, poinding of his goods, etc.) in the normal way.

(3) Where there is a personal relationship involved, *e.g.* a contract of service or a partnership contract.[4]

(4) Where it would be impossible to comply with the decree. The court would not, for example, oblige a person to carry out his contractual obligation to do something on or with property which does not belong to him and to which he has no rights.[5]

(5) Although probably a variant number of 4 above (impossibility), the courts will not pronounce a decree *ad factum praestandum* where the obligation sought to be enforced is too vague, so that the courts would not know whether it had been performed or not. This has been one of the reasons why the courts have been reluctant to enforce "keep open" clauses in leases: unless the obligation to trade is clearly defined, so that it is certain what the tenant will have to do in order to trade continuously, the courts

---

2   For an explanation of the distinction between Scots and English law in relation to specific implement or specific performance, see *Stewart v. Kennedy* (1890) 17 R. (H.L.) 1 at pp. 9 and 10.

3   *Grahame v. Magistrates of Kirkcaldy* (1889) 9 R. (H.L.) 91.

4   *Macarthur v. Lawson* (1877) 4 R. 1134; *Skerret v. Oliver* (1896) 23 R. 468.

5   *Sinclair v. Caithness Flagstone Co.* (1898) 25 R. 703.

may not know when a decree ordaining the tenant to trade as such has not been performed. Since the remedy is imprisonment in the case of an individual or a fine in the case of a company the reason for the reluctance is apparent. The Scottish courts have, however, recently enforced an obligation to trade as a bank since they were presumably quite certain what that meant.[6]

(6) Where the court cannot enforce the decree. If the person against whom the decree would otherwise be pronounced is beyond the jurisdiction of the court and therefore cannot be imprisoned for breach, decree will be refused.

(7) Where, in a contract of sale, the subject matter of the contract is generic goods which can be readily obtained in the open market.[7] This is an example of where a court would not regard it as reasonable to grant a decree *ad factum praestandum*. Damages would suffice in this instance. It would be different if the subject matter were a specific unique article which the contracting party refused to supply in breach of his contract.

In England, by contrast, the equivalent remedy of specific performance is an equitable remedy entirely at the discretion of the courts.[8] It has been held since the early nineteenth century in England that the remedy of specific performance is not available to a landlord seeking to have his tenant effect repairs in terms of a lease.[9] However, although that case has been supported by other English authorities, the authors of a leading English textbook on dilapidations doubt whether the line of authority is still correct.[10]

Landlord's right to do works himself and charge tenant

The landlord may have reserved to himself in the lease the right to **5.7** enter the premises and carry out the necessary repairs at the expense of the tenant if the tenant fails to comply with his repairing

---

[6] *Retail Parks Investments Ltd v. Royal Bank of Scotland (No. 2)*, 1996 S.L.T. 669.

[7] *Union Electric Co. v. Holman*, 1913 S.C. 954.

[8] For an explanation of the distinction between Scots and English law in relation to specific implement or specific performance, see *Stewart v. Kennedy* (1890) 17 R. (H.L.) 1 at pp. 9 and 10.

[9] *Hill v. Barclay* (1810) 16 Ves. 402.

[10] See Dowding and Reynolds, *Dilapidations — The Modern Law and Practice* (1995), p. 558.

obligations. In a well drafted commercial lease, the landlord will have provided for the tenant to pay interest, usually from the date upon which the landlord incurred the cost of repairs, as well as any professional fees properly incurred. If no such right is reserved, then a landlord will have no common law implied right to enter the premises during the lease to carry out such repairs and will have to rely upon other remedies. This is because the landlord has contracted in the lease to give the tenant exclusive possession of the premises during its whole currency.[11] In England the landlord would be committing trespass in similar circumstances.

5.8   In England, the inclusion of such a right of entry to carry out repairs has far greater significance than in Scotland for several reasons. First, as had already been seen, a landlord in England cannot apply to the court for decree of specific performance (specific implement in our terminology).[12] Secondly, where he is dealing with a lease for more than seven years of which at least three remain outstanding, a landlord in England cannot even claim damages or forfeit or terminate the lease without complying with the terms of section 1(2) of the Leasehold Property (Repairs) Act 1938. This states that a claim by a landlord for damages for breach by a tenant of his repairing obligation is, in the case of a lease exceeding seven years with more than three still to run, unenforceable, unless the landlord has served a notice under section 146(1) of the Law of Property Act 1925.[13] The 1938 Act then provides that the section 146 Notice must also contain a statement "in characters not less conspicuous than those used in any other part of the notice" to the effect that the tenant is entitled to serve a counter-notice claiming the benefit of the 1938 Act — and the requirements are very strictly enforced. If a counter-notice is served within 28 days of the original landlord's notice, the landlord is barred from taking any further action to terminate the lease or claim damages from the tenant unless, on application to the court by the landlord, the court allows the landlord leave to proceed. The court will do so only if the landlord can prove one or more of five grounds:

---

[11] See *Stair Memorial Encyclopaedia of the Laws of Scotland*, Vol. 13, paras. 249 *et seq.*.

[12] *Hill v. Barclay* (1810) 16 Ves 402.

[13] s. 146 (1) relates to forfeiture notices and requires that the notice must specify the breach, require the tenant to remedy it and require the tenant to compensate the landlord in money for the breach. The landlord must allow the tenant a reasonable time to remedy the breach and pay the compensation.

(1) that the value of the landlord's reversionary interest in the·
premises has already been, or will be, substantially diminished by
the tenant's breach;

(2) that the immediate remedying of the breach is required to
comply with statute or court order;

(3) that, in the case where a tenant is not the occupier of the
premises, the immediate remedying of the breach is required in the
occupier's interest;

(4) that the cost of remedying the breach immediately is small
compared to the likely cost of doing so in the event of delay; and,

(5) that there are special circumstances which in the court's view
render it just and equitable that the landlord should be given leave
to proceed.

Even if the landlord surmounts this hurdle and proceeds with the
forfeiture or termination action, the usual grounds upon which a
tenant in England can claim relief from forfeiture in general (*i.e.*
not specifically relating to forfeiture for breach of a repairing
obligation) will present yet another hurdle which the landlord in
England may have to surmount. The 1938 Act was passed to prevent
unscrupulous landlords purchasing property in poor repair, letting
it to tenants with a standard repairing obligation and then attempting
to have the tenants "improve" the property by carrying out repairs
which they could not afford. In order to avoid landlords having to
go through this cumbersome procedure, English leases have
specified that a landlord will have a right to enter premises and
carry out repairs himself at the tenant's cost (assuming the tenant
defaults in complying). Until recently there had been some doubt
as to whether this procedure was simply a device to circumvent
the 1938 Act which the English courts would strike down, but a
recent case has removed the doubt and confirmed the landlord's
entitlement to avail himself of the benefit of such provision.[14]

Damages

For damages to be claimed by a landlord, the tenant has to have **5.9**
committed a breach of the lease (in this instance the repairing
obligation) and the landlord has to have suffered loss. During the
course of a lease, there is less likelihood of a landlord suffering

---

[14] *Jervis v. Harris* [1996] 10 EG 159.

loss as a result of breach by the tenant of his repairing obligation, but it could happen if the landlord was in the course of selling or obtaining a loan on the security of his interest, the tenant had been made aware of the impending sale or loan when the lease was entered into and the disrepair prejudiced the sale or loan.[15] For damages to be recoverable from the tenant in those circumstances, they would have to fall under one of the two heads of claim for damages set out in *Hadley v. Baxendale*[16]: see paragraph 5.13. In the absence of special circumstances (such as that the tenant knew the landlord had a lucrative sale deal in the offing before the lease was signed and in spite of that prejudiced it by failing to keep the premises in repair), it would probably be very difficult for a landlord to show that his loss in this situation was recoverable. Normally, however, damages become an issue at the end of a lease where the tenant has wholly or partially failed to comply with his repairing obligation or his obligation to hand back the premises at termination in compliance with that obligation or, if it has been served, with the valid requirements of a schedule of dilapidations. After the expiry of a lease, a tenant cannot claim the right to carry out the necessary repairs himself (since he has no right to possession of the premises after the expiry of the lease) and must therefore deal with the landlord's claim, if any, for damages.

5.10   In England, the common law rule prior to 1927, was that the measure of damages at the termination of a lease for breach by a tenant of his repairing obligation was always the cost of doing the works. This rule was affirmed in the case of *Joyner v. Weeks.*[17] In that case the outgoing tenant left the premises in disrepair contrary to his obligations in the lease. The plaintiff proved that the cost of putting the premises into a good state of repair would have been £70. The defendant said that he was not liable to pay £70 because the plaintiff had not suffered any real loss and was therefore only entitled to nominal damages. The defendant relied upon the fact that while the lease was still running and he was still in possession

---

[15] See *British Telecommunications plc v. Sun Life Assurance Society plc* [1995] 3 W.L.R. 622 and *Credit Suisse v. Beegas Nominees Ltd* [1994] 4 All E.R. 803, both cases involving the converse situation where the landlord had failed to comply with his obligation to keep the building of which the premises formed part in repair.

[16] (1854) 9 Exch 341.

[17] [1891] 2 Q.B. 31.

of the premises, the plaintiff re-let the premises to a third party commencing at the termination of the old lease. The rent under the new lease was effectively a full market rent and contained an obligation on the new tenant to pull down and alter part of the premises subject to the obligation to repair. The court awarded as damages the sum of £70, being the estimated cost of repair, notwithstanding these factors. The rule was held to apply even if it was established that the landlord merely intended to demolish the premises and clear the site.[18] To counteract this manifestly unfair rule, section 18(1) of the Landlord and Tenant Act 1927 was passed, providing for England (it does not apply in Scotland) that:

(1) damages for breach of a tenant's obligation to keep or put premises in repair during the currency of a lease or to leave or put premises in repair at the termination of a lease shall in no case exceed the amount (if any) by which the value of the landlord's reversionary interest in the premises is diminished by the breach, and

(2) no damages shall be recovered for such breach at the termination of the lease if it is shown that the premises, in whatever state of repair they might be, would at, or shortly after termination, have been pulled down, or such structural alterations made therein as would render valueless the repairs which the tenant obliged himself to carry out.

Section 18(1) does not apparently abolish the underlying English rule in *Joyner v. Weeks*[19] but merely sets a limit to the damages claimable (under the first part of the section) and provides (under the second), that despite the rule, no damages will be recovered in certain circumstances. The date upon which the diminution in the value of the landlord's reversionary interest in the premises is to be established at the end of a lease has been authoritatively laid down by the English courts as the date of expiry of the lease. In *Hanson v. Newman*[20] Romer L.J. stated:

"Now where a lessor seeks to recover damages from his tenant for breach of the covenant to leave the premises in repair, the section [Section 18(1) of the Landlord and Tenant Act 1927] says that the reversion is to be valued. Of course, strictly speaking, there is no

---

[18] *Ebbetts v. Conquest* [1895] 2 Ch. 377.
[19] *supra.*
[20] [1934] Ch. 298 at p. 306.

reversion left because the lease is determined, and that indicates plainly, to my mind, that for the purpose of the section the freehold always has to be valued subject to so much, if any, of the term as remains unexpired."

5.11   In Scotland, it has been conclusively established that the rule in *Joyner v. Weeks*[21] is not part of Scots law. The case which established this is *Duke of Portland v. Wood's Trustees.*[22] The case concerned the failure by a mineral tenant to hand back the mineral workings at the end of the lease in a state of good repair and free from flood water. The pursuers estimated their damages as in excess of £70,000, being the estimated cost of putting the property into the condition it should have been left in at the end of the lease. The defenders claimed that the damages should be limited to the capitalised value of the mineral royalties which the pursuers would not be able to obtain, standing the flooding. In other words, what the defenders were arguing was very close to the argument that the damages should be limited to the injury to the value of the landlord's interest. Lord President Clyde stated:

> "The tendency of our law is probably less favourable than that of England to the formulation of judge-made rules for the assessment of damages; and I am by no means prepared to affirm that the measure of damages laid down in *Joyner v. Weeks*[23] is, according to the law of Scotland, the sole legal measure of damages in such circumstances as were under consideration in that case, or in the present. The measures employed to estimate the money value of anything (including the damage flowing from a breach of contract) are not to be confounded with the value which it is sought to estimate; and the true value may only be found after employing more measures than one — in themselves all legitimate, but none of them necessarily conclusive by itself — and checking one result with another ... If, for example, the defenders should succeed in what may or may not be an easy task, that, namely, of proving the true loss suffered by the lessor to be materially less than the more readily ascertainable cost of repairing the ravages of their neglect, it may be — but I am deciding nothing at present one way or the other — that they may be entitled to ask the court to restrict the lessor's claim. All that we can, and do, decide at present is that the capitalised royalty value of the minerals included in the lease, but as yet unwrought, is not the sole legal measure of the pursuers' loss."

---

[21] *supra.*
[22] 1926 S.C. 640.
[23] *supra.*

The most recent Scottish reported case regarding the measure of **5.12** damages in relation to a breach by a tenant of his repairing obligation at the end of a lease is *Prudential Assurance Co. Ltd v. James Grant & Co. (West) Limited*.[24] In that case the pursuers sought damages from the defenders and had prepared an elaborate schedule of dilapidations which established that they would require to expend a substantial sum in repairing and redecorating the property. The defenders attempted to argue that the pursuers' claim was irrelevant and should be dismissed because they had not included in their pleadings averments as to the diminution in value of their interest as landlords. In England, following the passing of the Landlord and Tenant Act 1927, the cost of repairs claimed by the pursuers would have been capped at the level of diminution in value of the landlord's interest at the end of the lease (so far as caused by the tenant's breach), but in Scotland this would not necessarily be so. Lord McDonald who affirmed what Lord President Clyde had said in *Duke of Portland v. Wood's Trustees*[25] stated:

> "I conclude that the pursuers are entitled, in the first instance, to quantify their claim by reference to what it will cost to do the work which the defenders have failed to do. If the defenders can prove that the true loss suffered by the pursuers is materially less than this it is open to them, on suitable averments, to do so. I do not consider that it is incumbent upon the pursuers at this stage to enumerate in their pleadings all the legitimate but not necessarily conclusive measures of damage, to check these against each other and to produce, as a matter of averment, a figure reached on this basis. They have produced prima facie a figure based upon the readily ascertainable cost of repair and it is for the defenders, if they can, to aver and prove that this is too high."

Joyner v. Weeks[26] is therefore not part of the law of Scotland. **5.13** Nor, of course, does section 18 (1) of the Landlord and Tenant Act 1927 form part of Scots law. The overriding question to be answered in Scotland is what loss the landlord has suffered as a result of the tenant's breach of contract. Accordingly, a landlord's claim for damages is dealt with in the same way as a claim for damages arising out of any other breach of contract since, of course, a lease is simply a type of contract. Damages will be assessed on the basis

---

[24] 1982 S.L.T. 423.
[25] *supra.*
[26] *supra.*

that the landlord must take (even if in fact he has not) all reasonable steps to minimise his loss.[27] Thus, he cannot sit back and bemoan the state of the premises and hope to recover not only the cost of remedial works but also loss of rent *ad infinitum*. The measure of damages for breach of contract is determined under two heads: first, such damages as may fairly and reasonably be expected to flow from the breach in the normal course of events (known as ordinary damages); and second, such damages as may reasonably be supposed to be in the contemplation of both parties at the time they made the contract as the probable result of its breach (known as special or consequential damages). This rule for determining the measure of damages has become known as the rule in *Hadley v. Baxendale*.[28] Under the first leg of the rule (ordinary damages) it is not necessary to prove that either or both parties actually foresaw the loss claimed by the aggrieved party, so long as it can be proved that the loss arose naturally or according to the usual course of things from the breach of contract itself. It is not necessary that the extent of the aggrieved party's loss be foreseen, only the nature of it. Under the second leg of the rule (special or consequential damages) it is again unnecessary that the extent of the aggrieved party's loss be foreseen but only the nature of it. However, under this leg, it must be proved that the special or consequential damages claimed were or might reasonably be supposed to have been in the contemplation of the parties at the time they made the contract, *i.e.* at the time the lease was entered into. It is not necessary under this second leg that the party in breach actually foresaw the loss, far less the extent of it, merely that he might reasonably be supposed to have foreseen the nature of the loss. It should be noted that the aggrieved party's right (assuming he has one) to damages arises at the time when the breach occurs (for example when, at the end of his lease, the tenant leaves the premises in disrepair contrary to the provisions of the lease). However, whilst the right to damages arises at that time, the amount, or quantum, of damages may not be ascertainable at that time.

5.14   Whilst it is easy to state the rule in *Hadley v. Baxendale*[29] (see paragraph 5.13), it is more difficult in practice to determine how it

---

[27] *Admiralty v. Aberdeen Steam Trading Co.*, 1910 S.C. 553.
[28] (1854) 9 Exch 341, an English case which nonetheless reflected the position under Scots law at the time.
[29] (1854) 9 Exch 341.

applies to the typical breach by a tenant of his repairing obligation at the end of a lease. The following propositions and illustrations may assist the reader:

(1) For damages to be recoverable, they must first of all come within one or other of the two rules in *Hadley v. Baxendale.*[30]

(2) When considering whether the damages claimed come within one or other of the two rules in *Hadley v. Baxendale*[31] the relevant time is when the contract was made and not when it comes to an end or is broken. It is what is in the minds of the parties at the time the contract was made or what would be regarded as arising naturally or according to the usual course of things viewed from the time that the contract was made that is important.

A possible but unlikely scenario might be that a landlord enters into a contract to sell his property for £150,000, with settlement, entry and vacant possession set for two years hence. It is made a material condition of the contract that the property will be in a good state of repair and that the purchaser will obtain vacant possession by no later than the specified date, time being of the essence. In the meantime, to secure income from the property, the landlord lets it on a full repairing lease to a tenant and tells the tenant full details of the forward sale. The tenant fails to keep the property in repair and the market falls during the interval. The purchaser refuses to complete, the landlord loses the deal and has to sell the property for £93,000 (the market value at that time being established at, say, £100,000 for the property in a good state of repair). The landlord in that situation would not have had time to carry out the repairs himself which it is assumed would cost £10,000 and so secure the sale at the original contract price of £150,000, thus minimising his loss. His loss would not, as in England, be restricted to the diminution in the market value of his interest resulting from a tenant's breach of the repairing obligation (*i.e.* £100,000 less £93,000 or £7,000). Nor would it be restricted to the cost of carrying out the repairs (£10,000). The landlord in this unlikely scenario should be able to recover in full his loss of £50,000.

An analogous but perhaps more likely scenario would be a situation where the landlord has entered into, say, a year's internal

---

[30] (1854) 9 Exch 341.
[31] *ibid.*

repairing lease, of a shop in Argyle Street, Glasgow with tenant A to expire at mid-December and had pre-arranged a very lucrative six week Christmas let to tenant B at the expiry of the first lease, having told tenant A all about it before granting tenant A the first lease. If tenant A left the premises in a shambles and tenant B refused to proceed, the landlord ought to be able to recover the whole of the lost rental even if it greatly exceeded the cost of doing the repairs which he would not have had time to do. In England the most he would be likely to get by way of damages would be the cost of the repairs, and even that might be reduced if the diminution in the value of the landlord's interest at the termination of the first lease was held to be less than that.

(3) The landlord's damages for breach of an obligation to repair will normally be the difference in value between the property, as in fact handed over to him at the end of the lease, and what the property would have been worth if the tenant had properly performed his obligation. This may not necessarily be so in every case, and the case of *Duke of Portland's Trustees v. Wood*[32] is authority for the view that the Scottish courts are not as keen as their English counterparts to impose judge-made rules of universal application. This, and the fact that neither *Joyner v. Weeks*[33] nor the Landlord and Tenant Act 1927 hold sway in Scotland, indicate that, particularly in this area of the law, it is dangerous to rely too heavily on English cases although, on particular aspects, they may be a useful guide.

(4) In many cases, the cost to the landlord of carrying out repairs will equate with the diminution in the market value of his interest at the end of the lease, but that is not necessarily the case. A useful analogy is to be found in cases dealing with valuation of property, such as the case of *Martin v. Bell-Ingram*.[34] In that case the pursuers purchased a house in 1979 at a price of £33,500 based on a survey which indicated that the property was worth £35,000. Two years later, the pursuer attempted to sell the subjects for £48,500 at which point a defect in the property was discovered (a sagging roof). The property was eventually sold for £39,000. There was evidence that it would have cost between £1,500 and £2,000 to have effected repairs which would have left no obvious evidence of any defect.

---

[32] *supra.*
[33] *supra.*
[34] 1986 S.L.T. 575.

It was not disputed that when negligence consists of a failure by surveyors to detect a defect in a building, the proper measure of damages is the difference between the price paid by the purchaser relying upon the survey report, as representing the property without the defect, and the value of the property with the defect at that time. In fact the evidence as to the difference in the two market values which was produced to the court was assessed as at the date of the subsequent sale in 1981 but Lord Justice-Clerk Ross said:

"Of course these figures relate to a period more than two and a half years after the date of the sale to the pursuer. Nonetheless, I am of the opinion that the sheriff was entitled to conclude that there was no suggestion that the net diminution in value would have been any different at that earlier date. Moreover, the sheriff had regard to the evidence of repairs as a cross-check. Although the cost of repairs is not per se the proper measure of damages in a claim of this kind, it is legitimate to have regard to what repairs have cost ... In the circumstances of the present case, it appears to me reasonable to use evidence regarding the cost of repairs as a cross-check ... It is stated that the method of repair which would have left no obvious sign of any defect having been repaired would have been between £1,500 and £2,000. In all these circumstances I am of the opinion that the sheriff was entitled to conclude that, looking at the matter broadly, a figure of £2,500 was a proper figure to award for the first item of damages."

(5) The normal date to take, when assessing damages, is the date of termination of the lease at the point when the tenant failed to hand back the property in good repair. This is certainly the case where the damages are to be limited to the injury to the value of the landlord's interest. But as has been seen, the Scottish courts do not stick rigidly to any cast-iron rule but prefer to cross-check one measure of loss against another. They are normally sympathetic to "the more readily ascertainlable cost of repairing the ravages" of the tenant's neglect,[35] and it is well established that the landlord must take all reasonable steps to minimise his loss. He can only take those steps during the period after he first obtains possession. Repairs may necessarily be spread over a substantial period and it would be the cost of repairs reasonably incurred which would be relevant, and not what the repairs might have cost if they had all been done on the very day upon which the lease terminated. To

---

[35] *Duke of Portland's Trustees v. Wood,* 1926 S.C. 640.

take a simple example, if the tenant's failure to repair included a failure to renew lead on the roof and the price of lead at the date of termination of the lease was £X but by the time he carried out the repairs having acted reasonably the price was £2X, the landlord could recover the actual cost of the lead and not what the lead would have cost if he had bought it on the date of termination of the lease.

(6) If it is established that the landlord, despite the unrepaired state of the property (which he has not remedied) has been able to re-let the property to an incoming tenant at a full market rent for premises in good repair (and that he did not pay a reverse premium or grant a rent free period to compensate for the disrepair), then that new letting will not of itself extinguish the landlord's loss, for the loss will be the injury to the landlord's interest as at the date when the lease terminated. However, the fact of the new letting at no loss of rental will doubtless be exceedingly good evidence of the fact that, as at the date of termination of the old lease, the tenant's breach had caused little or no injury to the value of the landlord's interest.

Thus, in *Smiley v. Townshend*[36] premises had already been requisitioned at the time when the lease came to an end. At that time the premises were in a state of disrepair in breach of the tenant's repairing obligation. Although as things turned out the requisitioning authority did some outside decoration after the end of the lease but before the landlord recovered possession of the premises from the authority, that did not go to reduce the injury, as at the termination of the lease, to the landlord's reversionary interest. As Denning LJ. said:

> "[T]hat does not in itself affect the measure of damages … it is res inter alios acta. It is like the case of sale of goods where it has been held that a buyer of goods which are not up to contract is entitled to recover damages for the inferiority in quality even though he made a profitable re-sale and has in fact suffered no damage: see Slater v. Hoyle & Smith Ltd".[37]

In a later passage Denning LJ. stated: "But in such cases the subsequent event, when it happened, is not in itself sufficient to extinguish the damages. It is only evidence, albeit strong evidence, in retrospect, of the future as it appeared at the end of the lease."

---

[36] [1950] 2 K.B. 311.
[37] [1920] 2 K.B. 11.

In *Haviland v. Long*[38] the landlord entered into a new lease with another tenant before the old one expired. The new lease was at a full market rent (for premises in good repair), and the incoming tenant undertook to carry out any necessary repairs — but on the basis that the landlord would reimburse him out of the sums which the landlord might recover from the outgoing tenant for dilapidations. Denning LJ. said:

> "The measure of damage is the extent to which the market value of the reversion at the end of the lease was diminished by the want of repair. That depends on whether the repairs are going to be done or not. In cases where they have been or are going to be done the cost of repair is usually the measure of damage. The fact that the landlord has an undertaking from a new tenant does not go in diminution of damages. It is res inter alios acta."

In that case, the incoming tenant would not have agreed to take over liability for the dilapidated premises *and* pay a full market rent for premises in good repair without getting some reimbursement. In other words, the new bargain was *not* evidence that, at the termination of the lease, the value of the landlord's reversionary interest had not been injured.

(7) Where the landlord has not carried out any repairs and it is established that he is unlikely to do so, then it is highly likely that the damages which he will recover will be limited to the diminution in value of his interest as at the date of termination of lease.

(8) If the landlord puts the unrepaired property on the market for resale and if any reasonable purchaser of the property would demolish it regardless of its condition, then its repaired and disrepaired values are likely to be exactly the same and therefore the disrepair would not lead to any loss being suffered by the landlord. It should again be noted that the much more precise rule in the second limb of section 18(1) of the Landlord and Tenant Act 1927 (which states that *no* damages will be recovered if it is shown that the premises would at or shortly after termination have been pulled down or so structurally altered as to render valueless any repairs carried out by the tenant — see paragraph 5.10) does not apply in Scotland.

(9) If on the other hand, at the date when the lease terminates, there are no plans for demolition in existence but before the landlord

---

[38] [1952] 2 K.B. 80.

has carried out repairs, approval is given for a complete redevelopment, it will be a question of fact whether, at the date of termination of the lease, the tenant's failure to repair had caused the landlord loss. The court would have to determine what was the value of the property at the date of termination of the lease assuming that the tenant had repaired the property as against the value of the property in the condition in which it was handed over. If at the date of termination there was no likelihood at all of redevelopment, then the landlord's entitlement would be to the difference in value which was proved to exist at the termination. It might be that redevelopment was such a strong probability, although not yet formally approved, that the lack of repairs of the propery would not affect their value at all. However, if the possibility of redevelopment was a cloud on the horizon, the court would have to consider how the market in general would view the situation when determining what, if any, diminution in value had occurred.

(10) If it is shown that the landlord is selling the property for refurbishment rather than for any more substantial redevelopment, then it may well be that disrepair of the interior (for example, damaged partitions, etc.) would be completely irrelevant on the basis that the whole interior would be likely to be stripped out by the purchaser.

(11) Where the property concerned is a shop and the repairs concerned relate to areas which an incoming purchaser or tenant is likely to strip out as part of his shopfitting works, then again the landlord is unlikely to recover the costs of carrying out those repairs from the outgoing tenant.

(12) Where damages are to be assessed based on the cost of doing the works which the tenant has failed to do, the cost which the landlord actually incurred is likely to be good evidence of what the reasonable cost of doing the works would be, especially if the landlord can establish that he accepted the lowest of several tenders for the works. It is the reasonable cost of doing the works which he is entitled to recover (assuming the cost of the works is the appropriate measure of damages). The landlord has to minimise his loss and whilst he does not need to carry out the works using the cheapest of all possible materials and contractors, neither can he do so in a wholly extravagant fashion. The English courts distinguish between the type of works required to perform the obligation and the expense of doing the chosen type of work. Thus, if there are several satisfactory ways of repairing a roof, the person who has the obligation to do so is entitled to choose the least

expensive method (*e.g.* a patching job rather than a new roof).[39] And it is thought that where the landlord is seeking to recover damages assessed on the cost of carrying out works which the tenant failed to do, the landlord will also have to choose (or be deemed to have chosen) the least expensive method. He will then have to be reasonable (or be deemed to have been reasonable) as to the costs incurred in carrying out the chosen method.

(13) Again, where damages are being assessed on the cost of doing the works which the tenant failed to do, there seems to be no good reason why reasonably incurred professional fees should not be recovered.[40] VAT ought also to be recoverable in these circumstances where the landlord cannot reclaim it as input tax.

(14) Whether damages are being assessed on the basis of the cost of doing the works which the tenant failed to do or on the basis of the injury to the value of the landlord's interest at the end of the lease, notional loss of rent may figure in the claim. In the first case, the loss of rent will be what was or is likely to be lost during the time, which must be reasonable, it took or would likely take the landlord to carry out the works. In the second case, the loss of rent may form part of the injury to the value of the landlord's interest on the basis, for example, that a prospective purchaser would reduce his bid for the property not only by reference to what it would cost him to carry out the repairs but also by reference to the rent he would lose while carrying them out.

Whilst consideration of general tax treatment in the context of **5.15** damages is outwith the scope of this book, a few words on VAT may be useful.

(1) As has been seen, VAT may be a component part of a claim for damages for breach of a repairing obligation if the claimant cannot recover input tax (see paragraph 5.14, sub-paragraph 13).

(2) Customs regard dilapidations payments as outwith the scope of VAT. This will cover payments provided for in the lease, and payable at or near the termination of the lease, to enable the landlord to restore the property to its original condition.[41] Any claims for

---

[39] *Dame Margaret Hungerford Charity Trustees v. Beazeley* [1993] 2 EGLR 144.
[40] *Culworth Estates Ltd v. Society of Licensed Victuallers* (1991) 62 P. & C. R. 211. See also *Lowe v. Quayle Munro Ltd*, 1997 G.W.D. 10–438 where, although there was a specific provision for recovery of legal fees, the court implied a term that they must be reasonable.
[41] See Customs' Notice 742, para. 4.12.

damages not covered by the terms of the lease should also fall within this principle. This applies even if the landlord has elected to waive exemption from VAT.

(3) If under the lease the tenant is responsible for reinstatement of the dilapidations and the tenant engages a contractor, the contractor will issue a VAT invoice to the tenant who can then recover VAT, depending on the nature of the tenant's business.

(4) If under the lease the tenant is responsible for the reinstatement of the dilapidations and the tenant and the landlord agree that the landlord, on behalf of the tenant, will arrange for the works to be carried out, the landlord or the contractor will issue a VAT invoice to the tenant who can recover as in 3 above.

(5) If the landlord has not elected to waive exemption from VAT the landlord will not be able to recover VAT on fees and costs; otherwise the landlord will be able to recover input tax.

Irritancy or forfeiture of the lease

5.16 As has been seen in paragraph 5.8, the landlord in England has in most cases to go through the procedures set out in section 1 of the Leasehold Property Repairs Act 1938 and section 146(1) of the Law of Property Act 1925 in order to be able to terminate a tenant's lease for breach of the tenant's repairing obligations. There is then the hurdle of the tenant's statutory relief against forfeiture to be gone through by the English landlord. In Scotland, the only hurdle which the landlord has to overcome is the tenant's statutory relief against forfeiture. This is governed by sections 4, 5 and 6 of the Law Reform (Miscellaneous Provisions) (Scotland) Act 1985. Section 4 relates to monetary breaches, which are not relevant for the purposes of this work. Section 5 relates to non-monetary breaches, such as a breach by a tenant of his repairing obligation. It provides as follows:

"5 (1) Subject to subsection (2) below, a landlord shall not, for the purpose of treating a lease as terminated or terminating it, be entitled to rely —

(a) on a provision in the lease which purports to terminate it, or to enable the landlord to terminate it, in the event of an act or omission by the tenant (other than such a failure as is mentioned in section 4 (1) (a) of this Act) or of a change in the tenant's circumstances; or

(b) on the fact that such act or omission or change is, or is deemed by a provision of the lease to be, a material breach of contract, if in all the circumstances of the case a fair and reasonable landlord would not seek so to rely.

(2) No provision of a lease shall of itself, irrespective of the particular circumstances of the case, be held to be unenforceable by virtue of subsection (1) above.

(3) In the consideration, for the purposes of subsection (1)(a) or (b) above, of the circumstances of a case where —

(a) an act, omission or change is alleged to constitute a breach of a provision of the lease or a breach of contract; and
(b) the breach is capable of being remedied in reasonable time,

regard shall be had to whether a reasonable opportunity has been afforded to the tenant to enable the breach to be remedied."

It will be seen that the main protection afforded by the section to a tenant is whether, in all the circumstances of the case, a fair and reasonable landlord would seek to rely on his right of termination and that one of the factors to be considered by the court, in the case of a breach which is capable of being remedied in a reasonable time, is whether the tenant has been given a reasonable time to remedy it. It should be noted that the section only applies to leases of commercial or industrial property[42] and therefore that residential and agricultural tenancies are excluded from its ambit.

The latitude given to the landlord by the "fair and reasonable" **5.17** landlord requirement has been the subject of the recent Scottish case of *Blythswood Investments (Scotland) Ltd v. Clydesdale Electrical Stores Ltd (In Receivership) and the Joint Receivers thereof.*[43]

The facts in this case are, in brief, that Blythswood Investments, the landlords, were a property investment company which had acquired the industrial estate concerned to upgrade and improve as an investment for possible sale at a profit to an institutional investor. Units 6 and 8D were let to Clydesdale Electrical Stores who had in turn sublet the units at a profit rental. There being no averment that the tenants had failed to pay rent or service charge (which would have brought the matter under section 4 of the Law Reform (Miscellaneous Provisions)(Scotland) Act 1985), the landlords relied upon the "change of circumstances" of the tenants (*i.e.* their having gone into receivership) under section 5(1)(a) of the 1985

---

[42] s. 7 of the Law Reform (Miscellaneous Provisions) (Scotland) Act 1985.
[43] 1995 S.L.T. 150.

Act and the question for consideration was whether, in all the circumstances of the case, a fair and reasonable landlord would have sought to rely upon the provision of a lease which gave them a right to irritate or terminate it in the event of receivership of the tenants. The landlords submitted numerous reasons as to why a fair and reasonable landlord in their position would have sought to terminate the lease on the grounds of the tenants' receivership. Amongst these were:

(1) The leases concerned were not in the best current form of full repairing and insuring leases by virtue of defective features relating, amongst other things, to repairs, rent review, management and insurance. Termination of the leases would therefore afford an opportunity for better, more institutionally acceptable (and therefore more marketable) leases to be put in place.

(2) The rentals under the sub-leases were considerably higher than the head rentals and a new direct lease between the landlords and the sub-tenants or between the landlords and the proposed assignees (Scottish Power plc who intended to become tenants in place of Clydesdale Electrical Stores) would have meant that the landlords, rather than the tenants, would benefit. A fair and reasonable landlord would, as the actual landlords did, balance the advantage to themselves by taking into account the fact that, if the leases were terminated, the sub-tenants would have been able to enter into direct leases with the landlords at rentals not much above what they were paying to Clydesdale Electrical Stores and thus would have obtained better security of tenure; and the fact that if Scottish Power plc, as proposed assignees, had availed themselves of the opportunity to take new direct leases from the landlords, whilst they would have paid a higher rent under these than under the old leases, this increased liability would have been counterbalanced by their not having to pay a premium to Clydesdale Electrical Stores as outgoing tenants.

Lord Cullen took the view that the width of the words "in all the circumstances of the case" was such that he felt unable to reject the landlords' argument, and he accordingly allowed the facts on which the landlords based their argument to go to proof. He added that the issue was not whether the court considered what the landlords had done was fair and reasonable, but whether a fair and reasonable landlord in the position of the actual landlords and in all the circumstances of the case would have done what the actual landlords were seeking to do.

Whilst the facts of this case do not relate to breach by the tenant **5.18** of his repairing obligations, they do show that it may be very difficult for a tenant to overcome an argument by a landlord based on similar perceived advantages to the landlord which would accrue from terminating the lease. In the case of a remediable breach, such as a failure to repair would normally be, the court will also consider whether the tenant has been afforded a reasonable opportunity to remedy the breach. If he has been, and has still not remedied the breach within the allotted time, then the landlord's task in convincing the court that, in terminating the lease, he is acting as a fair and reasonable landlord would do in all the circumstances will be that much more easily accomplished.

A landlord also has to be very careful to ensure that, by his **5.19** actings, or those of his managing agents, he does not inadvertently waive his right to irritate the lease. Acceptance of rent or acquiescing in a breach by the tenant can result in the loss of the right to irritate a lease. In *HMV Fields Properties Ltd v. Bracken Self Selection Fabrics Ltd*[44] although the Inner House upheld an arbiter's decision that on the facts in that case acceptance of rent did not amount to waiver, they also stated that where a tenant remained in occupation of premises and tendered payment of rent when it fell due and the rent was accepted by the landlord, matters were being conducted in a way which was inconsistent with the lease having come to an end and that the landlord's actions, if looked at objectively, provided a clear indication that he was accepting that the lease remained in force. The question would always be a question of fact which would have to be answered in the light of the surrounding circumstances including the mechanism and history of rental payments. Lord President Hope also observed that there were significant differences between Scots and English law on the matter.

Tenant's remedies

The tenant has the following remedies for failure by the landlord **5.20** to comply with an implied or express obligation to repair:

(1) **Damages:** where the obligation relates to premises let to the tenant, the tenant has to give the landlord notice of the defect

---

[44] 1991 S.L.T. 31.

concerned and the landlord's liability for damages will not commence until the expiry of a reasonable period within which the landlord should have carried out the necessary work. Thus in *Wolfson v. Forester,*[45] Lord President Dunedin said:

> "By the law of Scotland the lease of every urban tenement is, in default of any stipulation, deemed to include an obligation on the part of the landlord to hand over the premises in a wind and water tight condition, and if he does not do so there is a breach of contract and he may be liable in damages. He is also bound to put them into a wind and water tight condition if by accident they become not so. But this is not a warranty, and accordingly he is in no breach as to this part of his bargain until the defect is brought to his notice and he fails to remedy it."

Where, however, the obligation relates to common parts in a building in multiple occupation, then, since those parts are regarded as being in the control of the landlord, his obligation to pay damages commences from the date upon which the repair became necessary. There is no need for the tenant to give notice of the breach to the landlord and the landlord may incur liability no matter how quickly he carries out the necessary repairs.[46] The measure of damages is assessed in the ordinary manner as for any breach of contract and has already been discussed in paragraph 5.13 and following in the context of a landlord's claim where the tenant is in breach. For example, in *Credit Suisse v. Beegas Nominees Limited*[47] the tenant was attempting to assign its lease of a substantial office building which was in a bad state of repair because the landlord had not implemented its obligation to keep the building in good and tenantable condition. If the landlord had carried out the repairs, the tenant would have been able to assign its lease for a premium of £85,000. Because of the disrepair, the lease could not be assigned. The English court awarded as damages the lost premium of £85,000 together with sums representing rates and other outgoings payable after the lease could have been assigned and rent, insurance and service charges which would become payable under the lease after that date.

---

[45] 1910 S.C. 675; see also *McKimmie's Trustees v.Armour* (1899) 2 F. 156.
[46] *British Telecommunications plc v. Sun Life Assurance Society plc* [1995] 3 W.L.R. 622, cited with approval in *Taylor Woodrow Property Company Ltd v. Strathclyde Regional Council,* 1996 G.W.D. 7–397.
[47] [1994] 4 All E.R. 803.

(2) **Specific implement:** if the landlord fails to carry out the necessary repairs, the tenant can seek a decree of specific implement which ordains the landlord to carry out the work. This remedy, in the context of a landlord seeking to enforce the tenant's obligation, has already been discussed in paragraph 5.6. Interestingly, although the English courts do not allow the landlord to use the equivalent English remedy of specific performance against the tenant, they do allow the tenant to use that remedy against the landlord.[48]

(3) **Compensation or Set-off:** if the tenant wishes to have repairs carried out particularly quickly or if the landlord fails to heed the tenant's request to have necessary repairs carried out, the tenant may be able to have the repairs carried out himself and set-off the cost against future payments of rent. A tenant has the right to do this at common law but this right may be restricted by the express provisions of the particular lease.[49]

(4) **Termination of the lease:** although landlords have the ultimate remedy of irritancy or forfeiture of the lease, if the lease so provides (and possibly also if there is no specific provision in a case where the tenant is in fundamental material breach of contract), there are no reported cases in Scotland of a successful attempt by a tenant to terminate a lease on the basis of fundamental material breach of contract by a landlord, *e.g.* a failure by him to carry out substantial and urgently required repairs in terms of his repairing obligations. In England, admittedly in a short three year assured residential tenancy, the court allowed the tenant to accept the landlord's material failure to carry out his statutory repairing obligations as amounting to "repudiation" by the landlord of the lease, and allowed the tenant to accept such repudiation and treat the lease as terminated by handing back the keys.[50] It appears likely that the Scottish courts might follow that decision as a result of *Scotmore Developments Ltd v. Anderton*.[51] This was a case where the tenant purported to rescind the lease on the grounds that the landlord had refused to consent to an assignation of the lease and, in so doing, had acted unreasonably and in material breach of contract, since the lease provided that consent was not to be

---

[48] *Jeune v. Queens Cross Properties Ltd.* [1974] Ch. 97.
[49] *Skene v. Cameron,* 1942 S.C. 393; *Glasgow Corporation v. Seniuk,* 1968 S.L.T. (Sh.Ct.) 47.
[50] *Hussein v. Mehlmann* [1992] 2 EGLR 87.
[51] 1996 S.L.T. 1304.

unreasonably withheld. In the event, the court held that the landlord had acted reasonably. However, the court expressed the opinion that the test of materiality of breach of contract was one which applied to the nature of the breach rather than the actual or anticipated consequences to the party founding upon it, although those consequences might be relevant as illustrating the materiality. They also expressed an opinion, provisionally, that any breach of a condition which compelled the landlord to act reasonably in relation to an assignation proposed by a tenant, or a joint tenant, went to the root of the contract and was therefore material. If, in a situation where the landlord is obliged to repair (which, as has been seen, is quite normal in relation to the structure of multi-let buildings), there is a very material breach of that obligation, it may well be that the court would decide that this was an obligation which went to the root of the contract and entitled the tenant to repudiate the lease and hand back the keys. The position would be even more favourable to a tenant of a building let on terms which bound the landlord to keep the whole of it in good repair with the tenant only being responsible for damage he might cause to the interior whether wilfully or by neglect.

CHAPTER 6

RESIDENTIAL LEASES

Introduction

As stated in Chapter 1, the common law relating to residential leases **6.1**
is substantially modified by statute, as opposed to that in the
commercial sphere. The common law position is, of course, very
similar to that relating to commercial leases, and it is equally
possible for provisions in the tenancy agreement to modify the
common law position. The statutory intervention now arises in the
majority of cases regulating the actual repairing obligations of a
landlord and is now found in Schedule 10, paragraph 3 of the
Housing (Scotland) Act 1987. It is expressly provided that these
provisions cannot be superseded by the tenancy agreement, and
the tenant's position is accordingly guaranteed by the statute.

It should also be noted that as a result of section 8(1) of the Land
Tenure Reform (Scotland) Act 1974 it is *not* possible in Scotland
for a residential lease (*i.e.* of a private dwelling-house) entered
into after September 1, 1974 to extend for a period of more than 20
years.

For greater consideration of the complicated issues arising, the
reader is referred to the specialist literature on this subject.[1]

Common law

As already stated,[2] a landlord is obliged at common law to keep **6.2**
the subjects of lease in a wind and watertight condition and to ensure
that they are in a tenantable and habitable condition, both at the
beginning of the term of the lease and throughout its duration. This
dual obligation is expressed succinctly as follows[3]:

---

[1] *e.g.* Robson, *Residential Tenancies* (1994); *Stair Memorial Encyclopaedia on
The Laws of Scotland*, Vol. 13.
[2] See para. 1.2.
[3] Rankine, *The Law of Leases in Scotland* (3rd ed., 1916), p. 241.

"The rule of the common law, as applied to urban tenements, is that they shall be put into habitable or tenantable condition by the landlord at entry... The landlord of an urban tenement is further bound at common law, *and unless it be otherwise stipulated*, to uphold it in a tenantable condition during the course of the lease."

The text in italics emphasises the possibility of circumventing these provisions by contract. However, due to the analogous nature of the recently enacted statutory provisions, there would be no real advantage to the landlord in attempting to deprive the tenant of these admittedly rather vague rights. To a certain extent, therefore, the common law has been superseded, but an examination of the exact extent of this obligation remains useful, since it forms a backdrop to the consolidation of the existing law effected by the 1987 Act.

Landlord's common law obligation re habitability

6.3 There is an obligation on the landlord to inspect the subjects prior to the period of lease in order to put them into a habitable or tenantable condition; the obligation, at that point, is *not* on the tenant to notify the landlord, and so "A landlord ... is obliged by the common law to put urban subjects in a habitable or tenantable condition at entry and that must entail an inspection of the subjects at that time."[4]

In contrast, throughout the duration of the lease, it is for the tenant to notify the landlord of repairs which require to be carried out to restore the property to the required tenantable or habitable state. The landlord is thus "not bound to inspect the premises periodically in order to see what their condition is, when he has no reason to suspect or believe that they are other than they should be."[5]

After such notification, the landlord is given a reasonable period in which to remedy the defect — what a "reasonable period" is depends largely on the danger to which the tenant is exposed by reason of the defect.[6]

---

[4] *Lamb v. Glasgow District Council,* 1978 S.L.T. (Notes) 64, *per* Lord Grieve.
[5] *Hampton v. Galloway & Sykes* (1899) 1 F. 501, *per* Lord Trayner at p. 507.
[6] See examples cited in Paton and Cameron, *The Law of Landlord and Tenant in Scotland,* p. 132.

Landlord's common law obligation re repair

There are certain situations where a landlord will not be under an **6.4**
obligation to repair the subjects of lease, for example, where the
need to repair is due to the negligence of the tenant — there has,
however, been recent litigation on the question of condensation
dampness,[7] when it was held that dampness allegedly caused by
a failure on the tenant's part to heat and ventilate the property
properly was in fact due to the landlord's failure to provide such
heating or ventilation. Defects caused by third-party actings are
within the tenant's responsibility, since the latter is under an
obligation to protect the integrity of the property.[8] Natural disasters
are a competent defence at common law to the obligation to repair,
but as this point will almost always be covered by insurance, it is
of limited practical use. A defence (open to the landlord) which
straddles the landlord's obligation to inspect the premises at the
beginning of the lease, and the tenant's obligation to notify the
landlord, is that the defect in question would have been obvious
to the tenant at the beginning of the lease. The case law on this
point dates from the first decade of this century[9] and it is debatable
whether a court in the 1990s would place this obligation on a
tenant, especially in view of the subsequent statutory development.

What is "tenantable and habitable" condition? This phrase is **6.5**
essentially reduced to the practical obligation to keep the subjects
of lease wind and watertight. The authoritative statement of the
law on this point was made by Lord Dunedin: "wind and watertight
means only wind and watertight against what may be called the
ordinary attacks of the elements, not against exceptional
encroachments of water due to other causes."[10] This has been
extended to a certain extent by later case law, most notably to include
rising damp,[11] since it was held that the presence of rising damp
made occupation of the subjects impossible, and accordingly they
were not of a habitable condition. The requirements for the subjects
to be "habitable" will cover anything within the subjects which
would be likely to endanger the tenant.

---

[7] *McArdle v. Glasgow District Council,* 1989 S.C.L.R. 19.
[8] *Allan v. Robertson's Trs.* (1891) 18 R. 932.
[9] *Mechan v. Watson,* 1907 S.C. 25; *Davidson v. Sprengel,* 1909 S.C. 566.
[10] *Wolfson v. Forrester,* 1910 S.C. 675 at p. 680.
[11] *Gunn v. National Coal Board,* 1982 S.L.T. 526.

A possible means of enforcing the common law obligations on the landlord is by means of section 3 of the Occupiers Liability (Scotland) Act 1960, which requires a landlord to "show care" to persons, *e.g.* tenants, in the subjects of let, as required by an occupier of premises towards persons entering. See also paragraph 6.11 re enforcement

Statutory intervention

6.6 As stated above, the major statutory provision in this area is now Schedule 10 to the Housing (Scotland) Act 1987.[12] In particular paragraph 1 in respect of the landlord's obligation in respect of habitability and paragraph 3 in respect of the landlord's obligation, in respect of short leases, of repair. These provisions have such an importance in this area that they merit reproduction here in full.

Landlord's statutory habitability obligations

6.7 Paragraph 1(2) of Schedule 10 states:

> "In any contract ... there shall, notwithstanding any stipulation to the contrary, be implied a condition that the house is at the commencement of the tenancy, and an undertaking that the house will be kept by the landlord during the tenancy, in all respects reasonably fit for human habitation."

In order to determine whether a property is fit for human habitation regard must be had to the building regulations in operation in the area in question. The provision applies to houses rented out at less than £300 per week.[13] It also applies to *parts* of houses let out for less than £300 per week. It does *not*, however, apply when the house is let for more than 3 years on the condition that the tenant will put the property into a condition fit for human habitation.[14]

6.8   There is a wealth of English authority interpreting the phrase "in all respects reasonably fit for human habitation". One of the

---

[12] Given effect to by s. 113 of the Housing (Scotland) Act 1987.

[13] The Landlord's Repairing Obligations (Specified Rent) (Scotland) (No. 2) Order 1988 as specified in Sched. 8 of the Housing (Scotland) Act 1988.

[14] Sched. 10, para. 1(2) of Housing (Scotland) Act 1987.

leading cases is *Morgan v. Liverpool Corporation*[15] in which it was stated that:

> "If the state of repair of a house is such that by ordinary user damage may naturally be caused to the occupier, either in respect of personal injury to life or limbs or injury to health, then the house is not in all respects reasonably fit for human habitation".

It will be noted that this statement is not only relatively contemporaneous with the development of the common law obligations in Scotland, but was also, at least implicitly, followed in the decision in *Lamb v. Glasgow District Council*.[16] In the case of *Summers v. Salford Corporation*[17] a broken sash cord in the window in one of two bedrooms in a four-room house rendered the subjects unfit for human habitation, in the opinion of the court. In that case Lord Atkin stated that "a burst or leaking pipe, a displaced slate or tile, a stopped drain, a rotten stair tread may each of them until repair make a house unfit to live in, though each of them may be quickly and cheaply repaired." But disrepair to a single room would not be sufficient unless the effect was to render the whole house not reasonably fit for human habitation. It would appear that these English cases are equally applicable to the common law situation in Scotland, and Scottish authority dealing with common law obligations is equally applicable to the subsequent statutory enactment.

Landlord's statutory repairing obligations

These are found at paragraph 3(1) of Schedule 10 to the 1987 Act, **6.9** and are expressly stated not to be alterable by provisions of the tenancy agreement:

> "In any lease of a house, being a lease to which this paragraph applies, there shall be implied a provision that the lessor will—
>
> (a) keep in repair the structure and exterior of the house (including drains, gutters and external pipes); and
> (b) keep in repair and proper working order the installations in the house—

---

[15] [1927] 2 K.B. 131 at p. 145.
[16] 1978 S.L.T. (Notes) 64.
[17] [1943] A.C. 283.

(i) for the supply of water, gas and electricity, and for sanitation (including basins, sinks, baths and sanitary conveniences but not, except as aforesaid, fixtures, fittings and appliances for making use of the supply of water, gas or electricity), and

(ii) for space heating or heating water".

The leases "to which this paragraph applies" are any leases granted on or after July 3, 1962 for a period of less than seven years.[18] The rent payable under a lease is immaterial for inclusion in these provisions. Such included leases comprise those which can be terminated by the landlord prior to the expiry of seven years, but not a lease extendable by the tenant to a cumulative period of more than seven years, which the landlord cannot terminate prior to the expiry of seven years. In addition, any lease of part of a house, which fulfils the other criteria, falls within the ambit of paragraph 3.[19]

In contrast to the "habitability" provisions, (see paragraph 6.7), it is possible to vary the obligations imposed on the landlord by paragraph 3, but only with the consent of a sheriff. The application for this order may be made by one party to the lease, but only with the consent of the other.[20]

Judicial interpretation of repair

6.10 It is, of course, necessary to apply the statutory wording to practical situations and examine the judicial interpretation of the concept of "repair", bearing in mind the context provided by paragraph 3(3):

> "In determining the standard of repair required by the implied repairs provision in relation to any house, regard shall be had to the age, character and prospective life of the house and the locality in which it is situated."

6.11 The authoritative statement of the law on this matter would appear to come from the English case of *Morcom v. Campbell-Johnston*[21]:

---

[18] Sched. 10, para. 4.
[19] Sched. 10, para. 3(1A), inserted by Housing (Scotland) Act 1988, Sched. 8, para. 9(b).
[20] Sched. 10, para. 5.
[21] [1956] 1 Q.B. 106.

"It seems to me that the test, so far as one can give any test in these matters, is this: if the work which is done is the provision of something new for the benefit of the occupier, that is, properly speaking, an improvement; but if it is only the replacement of something already there, which has become dilapidated or worn out, then albeit that it is a replacement by its modern equivalent, it comes within the category of repairs and not improvements."[22]

This was later adopted by Lord President Clyde as an **6.12** authoritative statement of Scots law.[23] The water is somewhat muddied, however, by the English case of *Ravenseft Properties Ltd v. Davstone (Holdings) Ltd*,[24] involving commercial property where the correction of an inherent design defect was held not to be an improvement, but rather a repair. It was a matter of degree and in this instance since the addition of expansion joists was the only way the building could be repaired, the work was not an improvement.

However, "repair" relates to the structure and exterior of the building and is consequently quite a different concept from that of "habitability". It has been held by the English Court of Appeal[25] that condensation dampness, which caused damage to the decoration of the house and thus was detrimental to the amenity, rather than the structure, of the property, did not fall within the "repair" obligation. This case states that there requires to be tangible disrepair before "repair" can take place, *i.e.* the state which the house was in at the beginning of the lease must be manifestly different from that when the repair is contemplated. Redecoration, however, requires to be undertaken by the landlord when this is a necessary consequence of the carrying out of the repair works.[26]

The definition of "structure" and "exterior" was dealt with in a sheriff court case, *Hastie v. City of Edinburgh District Council*[27] in which it was stated at first instance, and affirmed on appeal, that (i) "the structure of a house is that part of it which gives it stability, shape and identity as a house. The essentials seem ... to be foundations, walls and roof",[28] and (ii) "the exterior of the house is

[22] *Morcom v. Campbell-Johnston, supra, per* Lord Denning at p.115.
[23] *Stewart's Judicial Factor v. Gallagher,* 1967 S.C. 59 at p. 62.
[24] [1980] Q.B. 12.
[25] *Quick v. Taff-Ely Borough Council* [1986] Q.B. 809.
[26] *e.g. Little v. Glasgow District Council,* 1988 S.C.L.R. 482.
[27] 1981 S.L.T. (Sh.Ct.) 61 and, on appeal to Sheriff Principal, p. 92.
[28] 1981 S.L.T. (Sh.Ct.) 61 at p. 62.

the part of the house which lies between what is outside the house and what is inside the house".[29] In that case, it was held that a window, whilst not part of the structure of the house, was part of the exterior and accordingly fell within the landlord's repairing obligations. In addition, this case held that the landlord was liable to repair (under statute), even where such damage was caused by third parties, *e.g.* vandals.

Notification

6.13 In respect of both the landlord's obligation regarding habitability and the repairing obligation, there is a requirement, analogous to that under the common law obligation, that the landlord be notified of any defects by the tenant in order to give rise to the obligation. It would appear that notification is required whether the defect is obvious or not. It was, however, suggested by Lord Dunpark[30] that the landlord could be deemed to have received notification where the landlord ought reasonably to have known about the defect. This possible exception is, however, expressed too vaguely to be of much practical use.

Enforcement

By tenant

6.14 There are various means available to the tenant to enforce performance of the landlord's obligations. To a great extent, such means of enforcement are equally applicable to the statutory and common law obligations and the reader is refered to in paragraph 5.20.

    (1)(a) The tenant can apply to the sheriff court for a declarator stating the landlord's obligations, whether under the statute, at common law, or by virtue of the tenancy agreement.

    (b) The tenant can in addition raise an action of implement in the sheriff court to require the landlord to carry out the necessary work to meet his obligations.

    (c) In the event of the landlord, following on due notice, failing to meet his obligations, the tenant can in turn carry

---

[29] 1981 S.L.T. (Sh.Ct.) 61 at p. 63.
[30] *Golden Casket (Greenock) Ltd v. BRS (Pickfords) Ltd,* 1972 S.L.T. 146.

out the necessary work and seek to recover the costs thus incurred from the landlord.

(2) Depending on the provisions in the lease, the tenant may be entitled to withhold rent until the landlord's obligations have been fulfilled. This may simply, however, be a quick route to precipitating an action for debt recovery by the landlord.

(3) Under section 16 of the Public Health (Scotland) Act 1897 a local authority may take action against nuisances which are "injurious to public health". This obviously overlaps with the common law habitability obligation, but an actual danger to health requires to be established. A simple state of disrepair which does not include condensation, dampness, faulty construction, etc., would not fall within the ambit of this section.

(4) Under section 87(1) of the Civic Government (Scotland) Act 1982, a local authority may serve a notice on a property owner to rectify defects in their property "being defects which require rectification in order to bring the building into a reasonable state of repair, regard being had to its age, type and location."

(5) Under section 87(3) of the Civic Government (Scotland) Act 1982, if a local authority considers that it is necessary that they should immediately repair a building in their area "in the interests of health or safety or to prevent damage to any property", they can do so without prior notice to the owners and proceed to recover the cost of the repairs from the owner.

By landlord

The landlord has open to him similar means to seek to enforce **6.15** repair obligations to the extent that they are due by the tenant.[31] Accordingly:

(1) (a) The landlord can apply to the sheriff court for a declarator stating the tenant's obligations whether under statute, at common law, or by virtue of the tenancy agreement.

(b) The landlord can raise an action of implement to require the tenant to carry out the necessary work to meet his obligations.

(c) In the event of the tenant, following on due notice, failing to meet his obligations, the landlord can carry out the work and seek to recover the costs thus incurred from the tenant.

---

[31] See paragraph 5.2 and following.

(2) The landlord, of course, is not able to withhold rent as he is the recipient, but he could, alternatively, seek to irritate the lease in the light of the tenant's failure to meet his obligations.

(3) The landlord is, however, unlikely to wish to invoke the procedures under the Public Health (Scotland) Act 1897 (section 16) or, the Civic Government (Scotland) Act 1982 (section 87), since these will bring him into conflict with the local authorities. In any event it is unlikely that any of these procedures will be applicable in the case of a failure by a tenant to meet his obligations, which are generally of a less material nature.

CHAPTER 7

AGRICULTURAL TENANCIES

The law relating to agricultural tenancies has been heavily **7.1**
influenced by statutory intervention, the most recent example being
the largely consolidating Agricultural Holdings (Scotland) Act 1991.
It is beyond the scope of this book to endeavour to cover the question
of constitution of agricultural leases, and interested readers are
referred to the specialist literature on this subject.[1]

Fixed equipment

Under the Agriculture (Scotland) Act 1948,[2] the rules of good **7.2**
husbandry include the obligation "to carry out necessary work of
maintenance and repair of the fixed and other equipment."
Depending on the date of commencement or the specific terms of
the lease, the rules of good husbandry may be governed by the
common law, section 5 of the 1991 Act, or the lease itself.

Definition of fixed equipment

Fixed equipment on an agricultural tenancy is defined in section **7.3**
85(1) of the 1991 Act as including:

> "[A]ny building or structure affixed to land and any works on, in, over
> or under land, and also includes anything grown on land for a purpose
> other than use after severance from the land, consumption of the thing
> grown or of produce thereof, or amenity, and, without prejudice to the
> foregoing generality, includes the following things, that is to say—
>
> > (a) all permanent buildings, including farm houses and farm
> > cottages, necessary for the proper conduct of the agricultural
> > holding;

---

[1] *e.g.* Gill, *Law of Agricultural Holdings in Scotland* (2nd ed., 1990); Agnew of
Lochnaw, *Agricultural Law in Scotland* (1996); Connell, Agricultural Holdings
(Scotland) Acts (7th ed., 1996).

[2] Sched. 6, para. 2(f)(iv).

(b) all permanent fences, including hedges, stone dykes, gate posts and gates;

(c) all ditches, open drains and tile drains, conduits and culverts, ponds, sluices, flood banks and main water courses;

(d) stells, fanks, folds, dippers, pens and bughts necessary for the proper conduct of the holding;

(e) farm access or service roads, bridges and fords;

(f) water and sewerage systems;

(g) electrical installations including generating plant, fixed motors, wiring systems, switches and plug sockets;

(h) shelter belts,

and references to fixed equipment on land shall be construed accordingly."

Common law

7.4 At common law, a landlord is impliedly bound at the commencement of the lease, to put the buildings and fences into tenantable order. "Tenantable order" would appear to mean a state of repair such that, if the equipment in question was treated with ordinary care, it would be capable of lasting throughout the term (or extension) of the lease.[3] The obligation of the landlord does not cover maintenance of drains.[4]

The common law obligation on the tenant is to maintain the fixed equipment in the condition he found it, except for ordinary wear and tear.[5] If the fixed equipment is subject to natural wear and tear and requires to be renewed, the liability for renewal is the landlord's.[6] If fixed equipment is *not* put into repair by the landlord at the beginning of the lease, or not formally accepted by the tenant as being in a tenantable state of repair, then there is no obligation on the tenant to maintain it.[7]

If decay to fixed equipment is caused by misuse or neglect on the part of the tenant, then it is the tenant's responsibility to repair it or pay damages for its repairs. It is a question of fact whether such decay has been caused by the tenant's neglect or the age of the fixed equipment — if the latter is found to be the cause, the

---

[3] *e.g. Davidson v. Logan,* 1908 S.C. 350.

[4] *Wight v. Newton,* 1911 S.C. 762, but *cf. Lyon v. Anderson* (1886) 13 R. 1020.

[5] *Wight v. Newton, supra.*

[6] *Johnston v. Hugham* (1894) 21 R. 777.

[7] *Austin v. Gibson,* 1979 S.L.T. (Land Ct.) 12.

landlord is obliged to repair, but with a right to damages from the tenant to the extent that he has contributed to the loss.[8]

Statutory intervention

Section 5 of the 1991 Act applies to all leases entered into on or **7.5** after November 1, 1948. The provisions of this section are deemed to form part of every lease, notwithstanding the specific provisions contained in the lease.

Leases entered into prior to November 1, 1948 are not subject to the provisions of the above section, and thus the respective obligations of the landlord and tenant are governed by common law and the lease provisions. Accordingly, a landlord under a pre-1948 lease cannot be forced to effect renewal or replacement of an item of fixed equipment worn out as a result of natural decay or fair wear and tear unless so provided in the lease provisions. Even when a lease is running on tacit relocation, the landlord's obligations under the written lease subsist.[9] It is, however, competent for the parties to a lease entered into before November 1, 1948, to seek to vary the terms of the lease under section 4 of the 1991 Act, where the lease is inconsistent with any of the provisions of section 5.

Landlord's liability under statute

The liability of a landlord is governed by section 5(2)(a) of the **7.6** 1991 Act — this provides that the landlord is deemed to undertake that:

> "[A]t the commencement of the tenancy or as soon as is reasonably practicable thereafter, he will put the fixed equipment on the holding into a thorough state of repair[10] and will provide such buildings and other fixed equipment as will enable an occupier reasonably skilled in husbandry to maintain efficient production as respects both—
>
> (i) the kind of produce specified in the lease, or (failing such specification) in use to be produced on the holding, and
> (ii) the quality and quantity thereof,

---

[8] *Macnab v. Willison,* July 5, 1955, unreported (1st Div.), cited in Gill, *op. cit.,* para. 116.
[9] *Macnab v. Willison,* 1960 S.L.T. (Notes) 25.
[10] This is arguably a higher standard than that of "tenantable order" imposed by common law.

and that he will during the tenancy effect such replacement or renewal of the buildings or other fixed equipment as may be rendered necessary by natural decay or by fair wear and tear."

It would appear that the obligation imposed on the landlord by this section is more onerous than that imposed by common law, since the existing fixed equipment on the holding, whether or not in an acceptable condition, may not be adequate for the relevant use(s) of the holding. It should be noted that unless otherwise provided in the lease the existing use of the holding is applicable and thus the landlord can be liable to provide fixed equipment and buildings for that existing use.[11] Accordingly, it is preferable for the written lease to make reference to the use to which the holding will be put, in order to limit the landlord's potential liability under this provision.

It should also be noted that the obligation imposed on the landlord by statute is in relation to a hypothetical tenant reasonably skilled in husbandry, and does not relate to the situation of the actual tenant and his needs and requirements for fixed equipment and its maintenance.

Tenant's liability under statute

7.7 This arises by virtue of section 5(2)(b) of the 1991 Act which incorporates into every lease:

> "[A] provision that the liability of the tenant in relation to the maintenance of fixed equipment shall extend only to a liability to maintain the fixed equipment on the holding in as good a state of repair (natural decay and fair wear and tear excepted) as it was in
>
> (i) immediately after it was put in repair as aforesaid, or
> (ii) in the case of equipment provided, improved, replaced or renewed during the tenancy, immediately after it was so provided, improved, replaced or renewed."

This provision does not vary the common law position as discussed above, since if the landlord does not fulfil his obligation of maintenance under section 5(2)(a), the tenant has no obligation imposed on him beyond that to maintain the fixed equipment in whatever state of (dis)repair he found it.[12]

---

[11] *Taylor v. Burnett's Trs.*, 1966 S.C.L.R. App 139, cited in Gill, *op. cit.*, para. 122.

[12] *Austin v. Gibson*, 1979 S.L.T. (Land Ct.) 12.

Contracting out

The parties to an agricultural lease may not contract out of the **7.8** provisions contained in section 5(2),[13] but after the lease has been entered into, the parties may agree that one party will undertake works on behalf of the other party and may impose liability to pay for such works between the parties.

It is questionable whether the statement normally encountered in leases to the effect that the tenant accepts the buildings and fixed equipment on the holding as being in a thorough state of repair and sufficient to fulfil the landlord's obligations under section 5(2), would be upheld by a court or arbiter, if it were patently untrue that the said obligations had been fulfilled. It is safer to proceed by way of a post-lease agreement, under which the tenant may agree in many cases to a full repairing obligation being imposed on the tenant. Section 5(3) provides that the lease must have been executed prior to the execution of a post-lease agreement, in order that the tenant will have the protection of section 5(2) implied by the lease, before agreeing to divest himself of part of that protection.

Any dispute under section 5 must be submitted to arbitration.[14] In the case of leases entered into before November 1, 1948, it would seem that section 60 of the 1991 Act would operate to bring disputes over fixed equipment before an arbiter.

The Record

The making of a record is vital to the success of claims for **7.9** dilapidations, and also for apportionment of the obligation to maintain fixed equipment.

Under section 5(1) of the 1991 Act, the parties are obliged at commencement of the lease to make up a record of the condition of the holding, for every lease entered into on or after November 1, 1948. That record forms part of the lease.

The purpose of the record, and the job of the recorder, has been described as the following: "to give such a description of the condition of the holding and its equipment as will convey to the mind of a person reading it ten, fifteen or twenty years later

---

[13] *Secretary of State for Scotland v. Sinclair,* 1960 S.L.C.R. 10.
[14] s. 5 (5).

a clear idea of the state in which the farm was when the record was made."[15]

At any point during a subsisting tenancy, the landlord or the tenant may under section 8 of the 1991 Act require the making up of a record of the condition of the fixed equipment or cultivation of the holding. Under section 8(2), the tenant may require a record to be made of the improvements carried out by him on the holding or those for which, with the written consent of the landlord, he has paid compensation to an outgoing tenant, or of any fixtures or buildings which, under section 18 of the 1991 Act, he is entitled to remove.

It should be borne in mind that a record made under section 8 is *not* deemed to form part of the lease, in contrast to one made under section 5(1). If the landlord or tenant requires, the ambit of the record can be restricted to cover only part of the holding or the fixed equipment on the holding.

Enforcement

7.10 Where any question arises between a landlord and a tenant as to the liability of the landlord or tenant as the case may be, for the repair of fixed equipment on a holding, it requires to be determined by arbitration under section 5 of the 1991 Act.[16] (It should be noted that this does not apply to leases entered into before November 1, 1948.)

In the English case of *Turtian v. Johnston*[17] it was held in respect of the equivalent English provision that the "compulsory arbitration provisions apply ... up to the stage of establishing (a) obligation and (b) breach of obligation." The jurisdiction of the courts then come into play to order specific performance of the obligation or award damages in lieu.

The arbiter, however, having regard to any provision in his award, may vary the rent on the holding if it is equitable to do so.[18]

If an arbiter under section 4 of the 1991 Act transfers liability for the maintenance or repair of fixed equipment from the tenant

---

[15] Marshall, *Agricultural Outgoing Claims*, p. 219, quoted in Agnew of Lochnaw, *op. cit.*, p. 56.
[16] s. 5 (5).
[17] [1993] 2 All E.R. 673.
[18] s. 14 (1).

to the landlord, the arbiter may be required by the landlord to fix the compensation payable by the tenant to the landlord for past failures by the tenant to meet his repair obligations.[19]

Statutory compensation for landlord for deterioration, etc.

This arises at the end of the tenancy and is governed by section 45 **7.11** of the 1991 Act, the relevant provisions of which are as follows:

"(1) The landlord ... shall be entitled to recover from the tenant, on his quitting the holding on termination of the land tenancy compensation—

(a) where the landlord shows that the value of the holding has been reduced by dilapidation, deterioration or damage caused by;

(b) where dilapidation, deterioration or damage has been caused to any part of the holding or to anything in or on the holding by;

non-fulfilment by the tenant of his responsibilities to farm in accordance with the rules of good husbandry.

(2) The amount of compensation payable under subsection (1) above shall be

(a) where paragraph (a) of that subsection applies, (insofar as the landlord is not compensated for the dilapidation, deterioration or damage under paragraph (b) hereof) an amount equal to the reduction in the value of the holding;

(b) when paragraph (b) of this subsection applies, the cost, as at the date of the tenant's quitting the holding, of making good the dilapidation, deterioration or damage.

(3) Notwithstanding anything in this Act, the landlord may, in lieu of claiming compensation under section 1(b) above, claim compensation in respect of matters specified therein, under and in accordance with a lease in writing, so however that —

(a) compensation shall be so claimed only on the tenant's quitting the holding on the termination of the tenancy;

(b) subject to section 46(4) of this Act compensation shall not be claimed in respect of any one holding both under such a lease and under subsection (1) above;

and compensation under this subsection shall be treated, for the purposes of subsection 2(a) above and of section 46(2) of this Act as compensation under subsection 1(b) above."

---

[19] s. 46 (2).

It will therefore be seen that the landlord has a choice — whether to claim compensation under statute (*i.e.* subsection (1)), or under the tenancy agreement (*i.e.* subsection (3)), but both alternatives are subject to the requirement that a record of condition of the holding has been made up in accordance with section 5(1) or 8.[20] A landlord is, however, able to claim compensation from an earlier tenancy where the tenant has occupied the holding by virtue of two or more successive tenancies.[21] No claim for compensation will, however, lie in respect of the period of the tenancy prior to the making up of the record.[22]

It must be noted that, under section 45, compensation can only be gained for dilapidation or deterioration which is attributable to a failure on the tenant's part to respect the rules of good husbandry.

The above statutory provision mentions both "dilapidation" and "deterioration": whilst these are undoubtedly conceptually distinct, it has been held that specific "dilapidations" on the holding (specific failures by the tenant to keep the holding in a tenantable condition) could amount to a general deterioration of the holding.[23] Writers on the subject have suggested that dilapidations could specifically include "failure to repair gates, fences, drains, buildings, roads, ditches etc in breach of a term of the tenancy".[24]

Contrast of sections 45(1)(a) and 45(1)(b)

7.12 Sections 45(1)(a) and (b) of the 1991 Act represent distinct heads of claim: in most cases, a claim will lie under subsection (b), and a further claim could be made under subsection (a) for the reduction in value of the holding attributable to such dilapidations, deteriorations or damage. It should be noted that the landlord may only recover under subsection (a) under deduction of the amount recovered under subsection (b).[25] The amount of damages which can be claimed under subsection (b) is defined in the statute as the cost, as at the date of the tenant's quitting the holding, of making

---

[20] *Douglas v. Cassillis and Culzean Estates,* 1944 S.C. 355.

[21] s. 47(5).

[22] s. 47(3)(b) — by virtue of s. 47(3)(c), this is the date of the first record if more than one has been made.

[23] *Evans v. Jones* [1955] 2 Q.B. 58.

[24] p. 341 Scammell and Densham, *Law of Agricultural Holdings* (1989), quoted in Agnew of Lochnaw, *op. cit.,* p. 245.

[25] See generally, s. 45(2).

good the dilapidation, deterioration or damage. The position under subsection (a) is less clear — it has been suggested that damages will be equal to the loss of rental value during the time for the defects to be remedied and alternatively that the landlord's claim lies in respect of the expenditure required to bring the holding back to proper condition, *and* the loss incurred during the time taken for the defects to be remedied. The landlord may either retain the land until the remedial works have taken place, or re-let the land at a lower rent, where the remedial work may be a tenant's improvement with compensation payable on termination of the tenancy. The landlord will probably only be able to recover the amount arising through the course of action which would minimise his loss.

Compensation for landlord under lease for deterioration, etc.

In lieu of compensation claimed under section 45(1)(b), a landlord **7.13** can claim compensation under the provisions of the lease, on the tenant quitting the property at the termination of the lease.[26] It would appear that a claim under this provision still allows the landlord the general claim under section 45(1)(a), as outlined above. If the lease under which compensation is claimed was entered into after November 1, 1948, a record under section 5(1) or 8 must have been prepared.

Time-limits

There are strict time-limits which must be adhered to for the service **7.14** of notices intimating claims for compensation. In contrast to other notice periods under the Act, the time-limit for claims under section 45[27] runs in relation to the termination of the *tenancy* not the termination of occupancy. Under section 47(1), these claims must be intimated not later than three months *before* the termination of the tenancy. Section 62(2) does *not* apply to this provision to enable the notice period to be extended.[28] Section 47, accordingly, effectively prevents compensation being claimed in respect of dilapidations arising in the last three months of the lease.

---

[26] s. 45(3).
[27] *i.e.* not under the lease.
[28] *Coutts v. Barclay-Harvey,* 1956 S.L.T. (Sh.Ct.) 54 .

If, however, a claim is made under the lease itself, *e.g.* by virtue of section 45(3), then the time-limit for notice is two months *after* the termination of the tenancy.[29]

---

[29] s. 62(2).

INDEX